The call of the believer doesn't stop when we leave our home or exit the church doors. To the contrary, God's people have been commissioned to serve Him faithfully every moment of the day and in each sphere of our lives – including in our respective workplaces. In Shine, Kris DenBesten offers a framework fo⁓ ⁓he Lord's ambassadors wherever we live a⁓ ⁓

n Daly

⁓ ⁓ne Family

Imagine if Christian business leaders would make a commitment to daily live out the fundamentals of their faith at work and at home. Talk about a serious game changer! In fact, doing that could change the world. *SHINE* is an enlightening call to sharpen our focus on what really matters in life. It provides a game plan that not only leads to success today but ultimately impacts eternity. I highly recommend you read it.

**Bill McCartney**
Promise Keepers Founder and Chairman Emeritus
NCAA Hall of Fame Football Coach

I met Kris through reading the original version of *SHINE* years ago. I was pleased to recommend it to all our C12 Group members. Now I have had the privilege to preview the new and revised edition of *SHINE*, and it is even better! A must-read for every Christian business owner and leader. Well done, Kris.

**Buck Jacobs**
Founder, C12 Group

At Interstate Batteries, values and principles play a critical role in directing all our business decisions. In *SHINE*, Kris DenBesten reveals a powerful message about how godly values can significantly impact not only our work but also our lives and the lives of others. I recommend this book to anyone who wants their work to truly matter...forever.

**Norm Miller**
Chairman, Interstate Batteries

If you struggle in getting your team to work in harmony and desire to build a culture within your organization that honors God, you must read *SHINE*! Kris DenBesten has not only told a compelling story about his own journey; he also has provided a road map for you to develop and implement core values within your business. The book is practical, engaging, and full of inspiring stories that will motivate you to go build your own culture that becomes a beacon of light to your community.

**Rick Boxx**
Founder and CEO, Unconventional Business Network

In the workplace today, many people are looking for more significance in their work. Many have questions about how to integrate their faith into their work. This book gives inspirational guidance on how to integrate faith and work on a daily basis. It also challenges readers to find true significance and servanthood in their daily life and work.

**Mary Vermeer Andringa**
President/CEO, Vermeer Corporation
www.vermeer.com

This book should be a helpful tool for anyone who is a committed follower of Jesus Christ and desires to integrate the claims of their faith with the demands of their work.

**Bill Pollard**
Chairman Emeritus, ServiceMaster
Author, *Soul of the Firm* and
*Serving Two Masters*

Every business matters to God, and every employee and leadership in the marketplace has eternal consequences. *SHINE* will awaken a leader to a grander vision of what is possible with helpful principles, case studies, and guidance on how to build a great business that unlocks a greater purpose. Kris has lived this journey out and generously shares a story that can change your story to perhaps discover God's greater story for you!

**Mike Sharrow**
CEO, The C12 Group

Christian business leaders are uniquely positioned to shape the culture of the marketplace. This book, is full of practical wisdom, personal stories, relevant Scriptures, and powerful revelations that people can really use to improve their personal and professional lives. Reading *SHINE* and applying its principles will bring Godly transformation to your workplace.

**Raleigh B  Washington DD, M.Div**
President/CEO The Road To Jerusalem
President Emeritus Promise Keepers

# SHINE

### A Vision for Life and Work
### that IMPACTS ETERNITY

# KRIS DENBESTEN

Published by: HigherLife Development Services, Inc.

P.O. Box 623307

Oviedo, Florida 32762

(407) 563-4806

www.ahigherlife.com

ISBN: 978-1-951492-96-0
LOC Application #1-9137148551

For Worldwide Distribution, Printed in the USA
1 2 3 4 5 6 7 8 9 10 11

# CONTENTS

Introduction: The SHINE Vision . . . . . . . . . . . . . . . . . . . . . . . . . . . . . . . . . . .1

PRINCIPLE ONE: SERVE OTHERS

    Chapter 1:  Ignite the Flame of Servanthood . . . . . . . . . . . . . . . . . . . . .7

    Chapter 2:  Shine With Humility . . . . . . . . . . . . . . . . . . . . . . . . . . . . 17

    Chapter 3:  Shine With Compassion . . . . . . . . . . . . . . . . . . . . . . . . 27

    Chapter 4:  Shine With Generosity. . . . . . . . . . . . . . . . . . . . . . . . . . 37

PRINCIPLE TWO: HONOR GOD

    Chapter 5:  Ignite the Flame of Faithfulness . . . . . . . . . . . . . . . . . . . 49

    Chapter 6:  Shine With Trust. . . . . . . . . . . . . . . . . . . . . . . . . . . . . . 57

    Chapter 7:  Shine With Gratitude. . . . . . . . . . . . . . . . . . . . . . . . . . . 67

    Chapter 8:  Shine With Stewardship. . . . . . . . . . . . . . . . . . . . . . . . . 75

PRINCIPLE THREE: IMPROVE CONTINUALLY

    Chapter 9:  Ignite the Flame of Excellence . . . . . . . . . . . . . . . . . . . . 87

    Chapter 10:  Shine With Competence . . . . . . . . . . . . . . . . . . . . . . . . 95

    Chapter 11:  Shine With Courage. . . . . . . . . . . . . . . . . . . . . . . . . . . 103

    Chapter 12:  Shine With Passion. . . . . . . . . . . . . . . . . . . . . . . . . . . 111

PRINCIPLE FOUR: NAVIGATE BY VALUES

    Chapter 13:  Ignite the Flame of Integrity . . . . . . . . . . . . . . . . . . . . 123

    Chapter 14:  Shine With Clarity . . . . . . . . . . . . . . . . . . . . . . . . . . . 131

    Chapter 15:  Shine With Conviction . . . . . . . . . . . . . . . . . . . . . . . . 141

    Chapter 16:  Shine With Confidence . . . . . . . . . . . . . . . . . . . . . . . . 149

PRINCIPLE FIVE: EXCEL IN RELATIONSHIPS

    Chapter 17:  Ignite the Flame of Relationships. . . . . . . . . . . . . . . . . 161

    Chapter 18:  Shine With Credibility. . . . . . . . . . . . . . . . . . . . . . . . . 171

    Chapter 19:  Shine With Perseverance. . . . . . . . . . . . . . . . . . . . . . . . 179

    Chapter 20:  Shine With Love. . . . . . . . . . . . . . . . . . . . . . . . . . . . . 189

Conclusion:  Shine On!. . . . . . . . . . . . . . . . . . . . . . . . . . . . . . . . . . . 199

About the Author . . . . . . . . . . . . . . . . . . . . . . . . . . . . . . . . . . . . . . . . . . 205

# The SHINE Vision

*Where there is no vision the people perish:*
*but he that keepeth the law happy is he.*

—Proverbs 29:18 KJV

I remember reading this proverb in a book about casting vision. At the time, I was struggling to get by and going nowhere in my career. The book challenged me to look ahead, see a desired outcome, and do whatever it would take to reach that destination. *Having a vision is to be motivated by what could be rather than being held back by what is.*

Fueled by vision, my career took off. I climbed through the ranks and into corporate leadership. In the process, our annual revenues grew from around $6 million a year to more than $150 million. I eventually became the CEO and majority shareholder of our organization. Yet something was missing.

My misinterpretation of vision had me pursuing good things; however, in doing so, I was missing out on God's best. Even worse, my drive to succeed was so all-consuming that at one point, I realized my work had become my god. Something needed to change. Turning to the One True God for wisdom, I began to grasp what this proverb about vision really means. Where there is no instruction in the Word of God, people will walk in darkness and eventually be lost.

My vision was leading me down a path to darkness. Thankfully, the Lord redirected my journey with one word—SHINE. Instead of pursuing a Kris vision, I needed to seek a Kingdom vision for my work—rooted in God's Word—that would lead me to His Light. Seeking a God-ordained, Kingdom vision is what SHINE is all about. Life happens step by step. The vision to SHINE keeps me pointed in the right direction.

So how about you? Do you want to make a lasting impact? Do you long for a greater sense of significance, purpose, and joy in your work? Let me assure you, it is possible if you pursue the right vision. I pray this book will help point you to the Way.

# CATCH THE SHINE VISION

Perched on a breathtaking vista overlooking a shimmering sea, the leader cast a new vision to inspire his team. This vision would set them apart and lead them to stand out. While most followed established protocols, rules, and rituals, this leader implored his people to search deeply within themselves. His vision called for a radical departure from the status quo to embrace a revolutionary new way.

With unforeseen authority, the leader eloquently wove together the critical elements of mission, purpose, vision, and values. His words lifted the spirit of each person as he called for unquestioned commitment of heart, soul, mind, and strength.

This new way would not be easy. However, for those who would choose it, the benefit would reach beyond anyone's hopes or dreams. It would prove so compelling that, once embraced, this vision would shine on from generation to generation.

> *Let your light so shine before men, that they may see your good works and glorify your Father in heaven.*
>
> —Matthew 5:16, NKJV

Much has changed since Jesus cast this vision on a mount overlooking the Sea of Galilee. Yet the Source of light for this vision is the same yesterday, today, and tomorrow. We are called to shine— to live in such a way that others would see Christ's love radiating in us, to the glory of God the Father. We glorify our Father in heaven when we show His Son to those around us. Realizing this led me to prayerfully consider these questions: "What would it look like if Jesus came to work at our company? What are some key principles that would frame a vision of letting Christ be seen in our work?"

The kingdom vision cast by Jesus in Mathew 5:16 inspired me to write our company's vision statement: "SHINE with Excellence."

The following five biblical principles outline the SHINE vision:

- Serve Others

- Honor God

- Improve Continually

- Navigate by Values

- Excel in Relationships

The SHINE vision has become a beacon that guides my life and work. Corporately, this vision frames our culture, sets our priorities, and keeps us pointed in the right direction. Pursuing this vision not only inspires us today; it empowers us to impact eternity.

## THE SHINE VISION DEFINED

It is important to note that a vision does not define who we are. A vision declares who we aspire to become. A vision compelling enough to inspire others should clearly articulate these key elements:

**WHAT we do:**

- Serve Others:                    Our Mission
- Honor God:                       Our Purpose

**HOW we do it:**

- Improve Continually:             Our Vision
- Navigate by Values:              Our Values

**WHY we do it:**

- Excel in Relationships:          Our Eternal Impact

Consequently, the SHINE vision is not some how-to formula to make you the employee of the month, salesperson of the quarter, or entrepreneur of the year—although that could very well happen. Rather, it is a biblically based, Christ-centered approach for transforming your work from simply making a living to making an eternal impact. I am convinced that embracing and applying these principles will strengthen your character, improve your career, and lead you to greater fulfillment in all aspects of life. As you read this book, please note that SHINE is not something any of us can do on our own. We cannot shine for Christ in and of ourselves. Only He can shine in us.

PRINCIPLE ONE

# SERVE OTHERS

*For even the Son of Man came not to be served*
*but to serve others and to give His life as a ransom for many.*

—MATTHEW 20:28 NLT

## CHAPTER 1

# Ignite the Flame of Servanthood

*. . . But the greatest among you shall be your servant.*

—Matthew 23:11

It does not matter who you are—a lack of experience will not hold you back. In the same respect, advanced degrees and personal achievements are not prerequisites for pursuing the SHINE vision. The fact is, there is nothing you can do externally that will allow you to SHINE. "The Lord does not look at things people look at. People look at outward appearance, but the Lord looks at the heart" (1 Sam. 17:7b).

If you desire for Christ to SHINE in you, the heart is where it all begins. Jesus said the first and greatest commandment is, "Love the Lord your God with all your heart...and the second is like it, love your neighbor as yourself" (fr. Matt. 22:37–39). As believers in Christ, we are called to grow our love for God so we then can show His love to others. When this occurs, Christ's light comes alive in us and empowers us to SHINE through a heart of servanthood.

Successful businessman and leadership author Max De Pree said, "The first responsibility of a leader is to define reality. The last is to say thank you. In between the two, the leader must become a servant and a debtor.[1] Learning this concept has proven a powerful lesson for me.

Our company, Vermeer Southeast, sells construction equipment in Florida, Georgia, Alabama, and the Caribbean islands. During my tenure, we have experienced exponential growth, an accomplishment for which I took much of the credit. During those high-growth years, I climbed from salesman to sales manager to general manager and eventually to majority shareholder of our company. Along with my success came an unhealthy dose of self-pride. As the son of the company founder, I felt the added pressure to prove myself to everyone around me, including my dad.

One day, soon after I had been appointed sales manager, I closed the biggest deal in the history of our company. It was a multimillion-dollar deal to a customer who, up to that point, had bought exclusively from our competitor. Upon finalizing the order, I, filled with self-delight, waltzed into my dad's office and proclaimed, "I got the deal!"

He reached out to congratulate me. Instead of saying thank you, I grabbed his hand, looked him squarely in the eyes, and asked, "What's the biggest deal you ever closed, Dad?"

My father sat down in his chair and frowned. I knew he could not come up with a deal to top mine because there had never been one. Eventually his answer came, but it was not what I expected. "You know," he said, as he gave me one of those frustrated looks only a father can give his son, "I can't say that any particular transaction stands out in my mind. But I guess I take the most pride in knowing that this company has provided for so many families for so many

---

1. Max De Pree, *Leadership Is an Art* (New York: Dell Publishing, 1989), 11.

years and that God has allowed me to be part of it."

How could I respond to that? At that moment, I realized two important things:

1.  Humility flows from a servant's heart.
2.  It is far better to humble yourself than it is to be humbled.

I made no comment as I, ashamedly enlightened to my own arrogance, returned to my office. My dad had clearly defined leadership for me. My focus had been on looking in the mirror to applaud myself. If I wanted to become a leader, it would require looking out the window at others, serving them, and applauding them along the way.

. . . . . . . . . . . . . . . . . . . . . . . . . . . . . . . . . . . . . . . . . . . .

*Success is all about me.*

*Significance is all about we.*

. . . . . . . . . . . . . . . . . . . . . . . . . . . . . . . . . . . . . . . . . . . .

At that point, I began to comprehend the responsibility of serving others. *Success had been all about me; significance would be all about them.* For the first time, the correlation between greatness and serving began to resonate within me.

Serving others is more than just a good idea. It is a reflection of the heart. True significance is never found in serving self, but only in serving others. Success is all about me. Significance is all about we.

# SERVE PASSIONATELY

Occasionally, we applaud those who serve. We might say, "Thank you for your service." Yet we often view service as a duty or an obligation. This is a common perspective in the workplace, where we serve our time earning a wage. But why is this? It seems the typical workplace commonly fosters a "me first" environment.

In that setting, work can become a place of promoting self, climbing the corporate ladder, and looking out for number one. We serve to get ahead, make more money, and receive credit for our contributions. Work becomes all about us and what we want. However, when our service is all about us, we labor to make a living. Self-focused service performed out of obligation can leave us— like slaves to our work—empty and exhausted. However, we can change that by altering our perspective and applying the concept of servanthood.

**Servanthood suggests that we put others' needs before our own, regardless of circumstances.**

Our service is not controlled by our environment. Rather, it is a choice made in the heart. God places us in the workplace to serve others. He calls us to genuinely care about the needs, the dreams, the hopes, and the hurts of those around us. He wants us to see others as He sees them: as people in need.

**Servanthood has as its mission to glorify God by helping others.**

Our service, then, is no longer viewed as an obligation. Rather, it is an opportunity to do the good works God has planned for us. Our ultimate service is to God, who uses us to do good works that glorify Him. This provides us with a fresh way of looking at our work.

## Servanthood stimulates our hearts and redefines our focus.

A heart of servanthood is clearly committed to caring for the welfare and serving for the benefit of others. From this perspective, our acts of service can be viewed as blessings that we pass on to others. We no longer serve out of duty; we serve out of love that reflects the heart of Christ to those around us. "If anyone serves, he should do it with the strength God provides, so that in all things God may be praised through Jesus Christ…" (1 Peter 4:11b).

## Servanthood orders our priorities: people before profit.

In the simplest terms, for any business to survive, it must consistently accomplish two things:

1. Serve a need.
2. Make a profit.

For a business to exist, it must first serve a need. For continued existence, it needs to make a profit. For enduring success, a business must continually do both very well. It is important to note the order of these two essential elements. Serving comes before profit.

Profit is a lot like oxygen. You need it to survive. However, oxygen is not life itself. Likewise, contrary to popular belief, profit is not what business is all about. Servanthood defines serving others as the life of a company and that making a profit, like oxygen, sustains the company and allows it to continue serving.

In this setting, company leaders should seek to serve the needs of fellow workers. Employees give their best effort in an environment where they are served, appreciated, and cared for. When we put our employees first and serve them with sincerity, they generally respond by serving fellow team members and customers better. And that helps build strong relationships and boosts productivity.

· · · · · · · · · · · · · · · · · · · · · · · · · · · · · · · · · · · · · ·

*Most businesses serve for profit rather than profiting from serving.*

· · · · · · · · · · · · · · · · · · · · · · · · · · · · · · · · · · · · · ·

In business, the act of serving customers is of great importance. Leaders in most companies realize that if they serve the customer well, they will get more business. Consequently, most businesses serve for profit rather than profiting from serving. They serve the customer strictly to sell more product.

Servanthood requires more than that. True servants are motivated wholly by helping others. They do not serve for what it could bring in return, but rather for what it will do for those whom they serve. Servant-hearted employees choose to focus on how they can positively impact their organizations by helping others meet challenges and improve their professional and personal lives.

## SERVE UNSELFISHLY

Unfortunately, the workplace is flooded with those whose sole intent lies in serving themselves. Consequently, the concept of servanthood can seem foreign in today's business world. Can you imagine a company whose owners/leadership believe that their greatest responsibility is not targeting the bottom line but serving their employees? And what if employees, instead of focusing on their own personal needs and desires, began to look first at serving others? What if we all stopped focusing on how valuable we think we are and, instead, started focusing on bringing the most value to those we encounter at work? Think of the difference that could make.

In reality, this is exactly how Jesus directs us to serve. Scripture records His words and provides us with this great paradox of serving: "Whoever wants to become great among you must be your servant, and whoever wants to be first must be your slave" (Matt. 20:26–27).

Jesus made it quite clear that the way to greatness in God's Kingdom is not found in serving ourselves but in serving others. This servanthood concept is not given simply as the pathway for future Kindgom reward. Rather, it is given to us so we can embrace and exemplify it right now in our lives and work as we represent His Kingdom on earth.

## SERVE FAITHFULLY

God has equipped each of us with an unlimited ability to serve. In the process of serving others, we simultaneously serve Him. One of the easiest ways to prepare our hearts for serving others is through prayer.

If you find yourself dealing with a difficult customer or colleague, try praying for them by name. Ask God to use your interaction with them as a blessing to their lives. Your prayer can be quick and to the point...something like this:

*Thank You, God, for the person with whom I am about to speak. I pray that You grant us peace and that our interaction is mutually beneficial and honors You.*

It is amazing how much easier it is to serve someone you are praying for. As an employee, what greater display of servanthood could you show your employer than to pray for the company, its leaders, and your fellow employees daily?

Prayer is such a simple act of service, yet so often a forgotten one, especially in the workplace. Let me challenge you to give it a try. Whoever may cross your path today—a customer, your boss, a vendor, or a coworker—give thanks to God for that individual, and ask God to make your interactions with him or her a blessing. A quick prayer prepares your heart for service that shines.

. . . . . . . . . . . . . . . . . . . . . . . . . . . . . . . . . . . . . . . . . . . . .

*A heart of servanthood glorifies God by helping others.*

. . . . . . . . . . . . . . . . . . . . . . . . . . . . . . . . . . . . . . . . . . . . .

To understand service that shines, we need only look to the example of Jesus, who willingly stepped down from His heavenly throne and took on the role of a servant on earth. Through His readiness to serve the needs of others, Jesus revealed the true heart of God in servanthood. It is only through the purity of a servant's heart that Christ's light can shine in us. Inside each of us is a heart equipped for serving others—we just need to let it show.

A servant heart radiates humility to reach beyond ourselves, compassion to care for others, and generosity to help others find success.

> *Each one should use whatever gift he has received to serve others, faithfully administering God's grace in its various forms.*
>
> —1 Peter 4:10

CHAPTER 2

# Shine with Humility

## PUT OTHERS FIRST

*Do nothing out of selfish ambition or vain conceit, but in humility consider others better than yourselves.*

—Philippians 2:3

One of our regional managers, Manny, oversees sales and operations for our company in southeastern Florida and the Caribbean Islands. I know, it sounds like a rough job, but somebody has to do it. Right? Well, Manny is that perfect somebody to handle this responsibility. He is uniquely gifted to communicate effectively and build strong relationships in multicultural environments. He is a great fit for his role. The top character quality I would use to describe Manny is humility. Manny is one of those people who constantly reaches out to help others with a smile on his face. He shows that he cares by putting others first. Manny tells about his experience while working with our company:

> *Working at Vermeer Southeast has been a blessing for me. I love my job, but what is even better is how the vision to SHINE has impacted my life. Having a team bound by biblical*

*principles has paved a path for me to be open about my feelings and struggles in life. My team at Vermeer Southeast has helped me through some of the most difficult times in my life. As I walked through getting divorced and uncharted waters in my relationship with my boys, my Vermeer family has been right there for me. I would often question what have I done to deserve such hurt and pain. Fortunately, I have had a team at work who keeps my mind sound and my heart where it needs to be. I believe Christ working through others to help them through pain is exactly what SHINE is all about. The relationships I have at work have made a huge impact, not only in my career, but also on me personally.*

*I know that SHINE frames our work culture, but it also internally guides me. Because of the help I have received, I look at it as my responsibility to pay it forward—to help others in their time of need. This goes beyond my workplace and expands out to customers, vendors, other team members, my friends, and family. All in all, I seek to have SHINE to define my life by trying to put Christ first and following the principles of this acronym. It has impacted me for years, and I know it will continue for the rest of my life.*

There is more to Manny's story that is fairly unique. He once competed on the United States karate team and remains an expert in martial arts. Business travel has taken Manny and me to some rough places over the years. His friendly nature, relational skills, and peace-making attitude have given me great comfort in these instances. Not to mention, he is a good guy to have on your side if things get out of hand. Humility is a strength, not a weakness.

# LET GO OF EGO

In its simplest form, humility is putting others first. However, it is tough to be humble when our own egos keep getting in the way. Ego-related problems make it hard to be humble:

- **Inflated ego.** Too much pride leads to selfish ambition and fosters an unhealthy ego. Pride makes it difficult to put the needs of others before our own.

- **Deflated ego.** Too little pride limits a sense of self-worth and causes an individual to question how he or she could possibly benefit someone else.

- **Fragile ego.** Some try to mask their own insecurities by projecting a false sense of overconfidence, resulting in an air of arrogance or of self-promotion.

The typical workplace overflows with ego issues. Fortunately, humility is the best remedy for every type of ego problem. Humility places our focus on others and allows our egos to slip into the background. Regardless of the state of our egos, Scripture points to humility as the catalyst for long-term, significant advancement: *"All of you clothe yourselves with humility toward one another, because 'God opposes the proud but gives grace to the humble.' Humble yourselves, therefore, under God's mighty hand, that he may lift you up in due time"* (1 Peter 5:5–6).

*Good to Great*, the best-selling book by Jim Collins, examines good companies which, over time, became great companies. Collins's research reveals a fascinating fact: in all the top-performing companies, the good-to-great transitions came under the leadership of what he calls a Level 5 leader. Collins explains, "Level 5 leaders channel their ego needs away from themselves and into the larger goal of building a great company."[1]

---

1    Jim Collins, *Good to Great* (New York: Harper Collins, 2001), 22.

It was not the charismatic, self-promoting, bigger-than-life CEOs who led these top companies. Instead, it was humble servants who were willing to lay aside their egos to serve the needs of the organization. Level 5 leaders are defined by Collins as having a great mix of personal humility and professional will. They approach their work not so much for what it will get them, but more for how they can contribute to the overall cause.

*Be shepherds of God's flock that is under your care, serving as overseers—not because you must, but because you are willing, as God wants you to be; not greedy for money, but eager to serve; not lording it over those entrusted to you, but being examples to the flock.*

—1 Peter 5:2–3

# LET GO OF ENTITLEMENT

Face it: we all like to be served. Most of us crave the feeling of self-importance and take great pleasure when others serve our needs. Perhaps, in holding a title or a position at work that requires others to serve us, we begin to feel entitled to it. How easy it is to slip into the entitlement mindset. We believe we have earned the right to be served. Unfortunately, the tighter we cling to our own rights, the less effective we become as leaders.

. . . . . . . . . . . . . . . . . . . . . . . . . . . . . . . . . . . . . . . . . . . . . .

*Humility allows us to be the type of leaders God calls us to be.*

. . . . . . . . . . . . . . . . . . . . . . . . . . . . . . . . . . . . . . . . . . . . . .

If we have been burned by someone in the past and are feeling entitled to seeking vengeance, humility allows us to let go and not seek to even the score. Scripture calls for us to forgive those who trespass against us, no matter how difficult that may be.

> Get rid of all bitterness, rage, anger, harsh words, and slander, as well as all types of evil behavior. Instead, be kind to each other, tenderhearted, forgiving one another, just as God through Christ has forgiven you.
>
> —Ephesians 4:31–32, NLT

Forgiveness, at times, might seem completely impractical. Yet we are called to forgive others as Christ has forgiven us. This requires the humility to continually ask ourselves these questions:

- Are there perceived rights which I should let go?

- Do I need to seek forgiveness from someone?

- Is there someone I should forgive?

Forgiveness is at the core of a humble heart. Whether granting or receiving it, forgiveness is a freeing experience that opens our hearts to experience joy. We can let go of entitlement through the power of forgiveness.

# PICK UP JOY

Humility is a tough quality to live out. It demands that we relinquish our rights so we can take on responsibilities. When we relinquish our right to be served and willingly take on the responsibility of serving others, we not only become a more effective leader; we also open ourselves up to a much more joyful life.

As the CEO of our company, I carry a lot of responsibility for making decisions and getting things done. Based strictly on position, the view from atop the organizational chart often leads to a me-first mindset. Occasionally, someone will drop the ball, drag things out, or just not comprehend what I am trying to accomplish. In these instances, it is my responsibility to slow things down, clearly communicate expectations, and then hold others accountable to keep things moving forward. My natural tendency, however, is to take control and make authoritative decisions, regardless of other viewpoints. I reason, "I do not have time for this. I am the boss. They'll do what I say." True, this keeps things moving, and often in the right direction. However, this attitude is not a proper reflection of our Lord. In these instances, God often reminds me of the familiar acronym as a personal reminder of how to react when the grip on my rights gets too tight:

**J** — Jesus

**O** — Others

**Y** — Yourself

If we view our work from this perspective, the grip on our rights loosens and allows humility to shine through us. By focusing on Jesus first, we let go of our me-first perspective and take on the Christ-like attitude of serving others. Changing the focus from "me" to "we" does not lessen our responsibility in any way. It just leads us forward with a much greater sense of unity and teamwork. After all, the roots for a life of joy grow deepest in the soil of humility.

# PICK UP STRENGTH

Often the word *humility* is misconstrued as weakness. However, true humility provides great strength. It takes more than our own strength to overcome selfish desires and put others first. By humbling ourselves before God, we are in a position to have our hearts changed, tap into His power, and find the supernatural strength to serve humbly and confidently, regardless of the situation. If someone is rude or arrogant toward us, humility through Him provides Christ-like strength to remain upbeat and secure, despite their words or behavior.

Jesus displayed the perfect example of the strength found in humility.

> *Jesus knew that the Father had put all things under His power, and that He had come from God and was returning to God; so He got up from the meal... poured water into a basin and began to wash His disciples' feet, drying them with the towel that was wrapped around Him.*
> —John 13:3–5

It was from the position of ultimate authority that Jesus lovingly relinquished His right to be served and, instead, chose to serve others through the strength of humility.

## PUT OTHERS FIRST

A few years ago, the leaders of our company met to define our key operational objectives. With SHINE as our vison, we knew our first responsibility is to serve others in a way that honors God. To do this, we needed to define core objectives to guide us along the way as we pursued this vision.

We adopted the following objectives, which better define our corporate priorities of who and how we serve. We call these our four core objectives:

### Objective 1: Customer Loyalty

We will provide responsive service and caring support to nurture loyal relationships.

### Objective 2: Operational Integrity

We will do the right things, in the right way, and for the right reason.

### Objective 3: Revenue/Profit Growth

We will use profits to grow and improve, to provide for needs, and to affect our community in positive ways.

### Objective 4: Employee Engagement

We will empower our employees to reach their full potential by developing their talents and promoting their well-being.

. . . . . . . . . . . . . . . . . . . . . . . . . . . . . . . . . . . . . . .

*Serve others through humility—*

*put others first.*

. . . . . . . . . . . . . . . . . . . . . . . . . . . . . . . . . . . . . . .

Seeking these objectives takes the focus off individual agendas and keeps us working together. As a leadership group, we desire to serve God by putting Him first. It is not our intention to preach or try to force our beliefs on anyone. Yet we make it clear what we believe and Whom we ultimately serve. Not every one of our employees shares our Christian faith. It certainly is not a requirement of employment to work at our company. However, our corporate focus on serving the

Lord by serving others brings a sense of security to each employee, regardless of his or her worldview.

Consequently, a humble focus on people before profit, relationships before revenues, and others before self fosters continual growth, positive impact, and greater opportunities. Indeed, this kind of workplace proves to be a rewarding workplace.

## CHAPTER 3

# Shine with Compassion

## SHOW YOU CARE

*But when He saw the multitudes, He was moved with compassion*
*for them, because they were weary and scattered, like sheep*
*having no shepherd.*

—Matthew 9:36, NKJV

An effective way we show compassion for our employees is by
providing workplace chaplains who visit our locations to meet
with our employees on an ongoing basis. I believe this is one of the
most important benefits a company can provide for its employees.
When life happens, having someone available who is trained and
experienced in guiding people through difficult times has proven
invaluable.

Recently, one of our chaplains shared this story from an employee:

*A few months ago, my husband asked me for a divorce. My heart*
*was crushed, and my vision for my family was shattered. I took*
*a day off to mourn and cry. I was so happy when our chaplain*
*came by the next day at work. We were able to talk. Our chaplain*

*listened, and then he asked if he could pray. I said yes. He asked me if I was willing to fight for my marriage. He explained that if I wanted my marriage to be saved, I would need to commit to pray as well as to fight for it. I said, "Yes, I'll try."*

*After we prayed, our chaplain asked me if I would like to attend a weekend marriage seminar with my husband. He even offered to set it all up if my husband agreed. I texted my husband to call me. My heart was beating so hard, I could feel it in my neck. When he called, I just blurted out, "Our company chaplain has invited us to a retreat to save our marriage. I am willing to go. Are you?" When my husband agreed to go, I felt tremendous hope and relief.*

*The marriage retreat was more than an experience. It was a miracle! The whole time, I felt God's touch on me, my husband, and our marriage. I am so thankful that our chaplain stepped into my situation and helped me. He became the catalyst for God to save my marriage.*

All our chaplains' activities remain anonymous. We never hear about most. Yet I know there have been countless prayers spoken, guidance given, encouragement rendered, relationships strengthened, and crises walked through due to the compassionate service of our workplace chaplains.

# SHOW COMPASSION

Compassion reveals itself only when we show others we care. More than any other quality, compassion sets the tone for serving others. We might say we care. We may even act like we care. However, compassion reveals the true feelings of our hearts.

Our company is blessed with many outstanding employees. Each top performer is unique and brings certain distinct strengths and abilities to our team. Though these exceptional employees differ in many ways, one thing they all possess is the quality of compassion. Typically, the best employees in any setting are those who genuinely care for others and express that care by serving.

Instinctively, we all long to be cared for. It is amazing how customers will keep coming back when they know that you care. Conversely, a lack of compassion can cost any business dearly. Research by the American Society for Quality and the Quality and Productivity Center shows that 68 percent of customers who take their business elsewhere do so because they were turned away by an attitude of indifference on the part of the prior service provider.[1]

Smart businesspeople understand the important role that serving others plays in gaining or losing customers. The same holds true for employees. The most coveted work environment is one where employees are cared for, appreciated, and empowered to make a difference. Likewise, when employees know they are valued and cared for, they are more likely to value and care for customers. In business, as in life, compassion manifests itself when we cast aside our own selfish ambitions and genuinely serve others, regardless of the potential return.

Does this sound overwhelming? Here's a little secret: Showing someone we care is not terribly difficult if we really do care. *"Be kindly affectionate to one another with brotherly love, in honor giving preference to one another"* (Rom. 12:10, NKJV).

---

1   Lisa Ford, David McNair, Bill Perry, *Exceptional Customer Service* (Holbrook, MA: Adams Media Corp, 2001), 6.

. . . . . . . . . . . . . . . . . . . . . . . . . . . . . . . . . . . . . . . .

*Most problems are solved by those*
*who show they care.*

. . . . . . . . . . . . . . . . . . . . . . . . . . . . . . . . . . . . . .

Often, those whom we serve gain comfort by knowing that we care enough to try to help them. That is why so many problems smooth out almost instantly when we tune in to someone else's situation. Most problems are solved not by those who have all the answers but by those who show they care.

## KNOW YOU CARE

If we serve others just because we have to, it will show. Caring about the welfare of another requires an authentic attitude of the heart that shines through our beings. Compassion cannot be faked. It can only be sincerely expressed. If we have true compassion, those we serve will experience the following:

- See it.

- Feel it.

- Know it.

Think about a time you received poor service from someone. More than likely, that person left you with the impression that he or she did not care about you or your situation. A study by author and social scientist Daniel Yankelovich revealed that two-thirds of customers do not feel valued by those serving them.[2] Obviously, the heart of compassion is commonly lacking in today's workplace.

· · · · · · · · · · · · · · · · · · · · · · · · · · · · · · · · · · · · · · ·

*Others know we care only when*

*we show we care.*

· · · · · · · · · · · · · · · · · · · · · · · · · · · · · · · · · · · · · · ·

Years ago, I witnessed the following example in one of our own stores. A customer walked in the door and received no greeting. He walked over to our counter, where our customer service representative was busy on the computer. After pounding the keys for what seemed like an eternity, before looking up, our employee muttered, "Help you?"

As the customer began to explain what he needed, the phone rang. Our employee cut the customer off mid-sentence by grabbing the phone and screaming into the receiver, "Parts!" The customer then stood there and waited until the phone call was concluded.

There is not much compassion in that example, is there? However, before you get too judgmental, think about how often each of us is guilty of similar behavior. How often do we miss an opportunity to shine simply because we fail to show we care?

## BE PRESENT

"When I first came to work here, I did not like you. I thought you

---

2   Ibid., 7.

were aloof and stuck up. You walked around barely noticing and rarely paying much attention to us. But now that I have been here a while, I know you're not that bad. Now I know you really do care about others. Since you have so many other things on your mind, you just don't always show it."

I did not know how to respond when a young employee enlightened me with this information some years ago. I think she was attempting to give me a compliment, but it sure did not feel like one.

I am a strategic dreamer and a focused thinker. If not mindful, I can get all wrapped up in my own world and miss all that moves, breathes, and happens around me. This has proven time and again to be one of my primary deficiencies. Deep down, I genuinely care about others. However, too often, I fail to show it because I fail to pay enough attention. While it is my desire for each person I encounter to know I care about him or her, I realize that this will not happen automatically. It requires a conscious change in my practices to establish new habits when I am around others. This promotes my being more aware and giving deliberate attention to each person I encounter.

Having empathy for others is important for each of us. It is our ability to enter into, understand, and share someone else's situation. If we want others to know we care, it is our responsibility to show we care. Most people will not stick around long to find out if we genuinely do care. As a rule, they make that decision rather quickly. This often requires that we put our own thoughts on hold and simply be there for someone.

*Empathy* starts with listening intently. This is harder than it sounds because listening is so much more than hearing. The following techniques can help:

- **Engage.** Look them in the eyes and give them your full attention. Repeat things, ask for clarification, and reveal genuine interest. This assures that you hear what they say. It also keeps you focused.

- **Be open-minded.** Put your own opinions and biases on hold so you can fully understand the other person. This helps you draw people out more, and it prepares you to better express your own viewpoint when the time comes.

- **Wait.** Do not guess at their meaning, cut them short, or finish sentences for them. Listening is about them, not you. The more they say, the more you can learn.

- **Connect.** The best way to connect with the heart is by opening your ears. By listening with empathy, you enable their words to affect you and to connect with you at the heart level.

- **Be flexible.** Be willing to change your mind, if necessary. This does not mean you must let go of your values or turn off your brain. However, it helps to be less defensive and more open to adjusting your opinion—based on the information you get from others.

This kind of listening happens only when we are genuinely compassionate and willing to be present for someone. It requires that we put all other things on hold and give someone our full attention.

# DO SOMETHING

Compassion requires more than just a feeling. We can listen, understand, and feel concern. However, until we do something about it, we have not shown how much we care. James 2:17 tells us that faith without works is dead. In the same way, concern without action is not compassion.

How often do we say, "I'll pray for you," and then walk away without taking any further action? Although we should follow through by praying, authentic compassion often requires that we go beyond simply saying something. To demonstrate true compassion, we can follow the model of Jesus:

> *Two blind men sitting by the road, when they heard that Jesus was passing by, cried out, saying, "Have mercy on us, O Lord, Son of David!" . . . Jesus stood still and called them, and said,*
> *"What do you want Me to do for you?"*
> *They said to Him, "Lord, that our eyes may be opened."*
> *So Jesus had compassion and touched their eyes.*
> *And immediately their eyes received sight, and they followed Him.*
> —Matthew 20:30–34, NKJV

Notice in the passage above that when Jesus asked the two blind men, "What do you want me to do for you?" He already knew what they needed. Still, He asked the question.

Here are two great questions to ask those we serve:

- What can I do for you?

- How can I serve you?

Asking these questions communicates our concern, and hearing the person's answer provides the specific opportunity to respond with compassion. If it is within our power to meet someone's need, we should do it. Like Christ, we should connect with others, feel their pain, and do what we can to help.

# FOLLOW UP

One of the simplest ways to show we care is to follow up with someone to see how they are doing. If a fellow employee has shared something with us, our following up with him or her makes the strong statement that we genuinely care. If we recently have served a customer, a quick follow-up call, email, or text to check on that customer goes a long way. At a minimum, we should ask these questions:

- Was our service a good value for you?

- How can we serve you better in the future?

- Would you recommend our service to others?

Follow-up provides an opportunity to see how our service is playing out. It is also an opportunity to learn and improve. Most importantly, follow-up clearly communicates how much we care.

The formula for showing compassion is simple:

1. Ask.

2. Listen.

3. Empathize.

4. Take action.

5. Follow up.

Whether it is lending a hand, lending an ear, or lending support, do what you can to help improve someone else's situation. Shine with compassion. Show you care.

## CHAPTER 4

# Shine with Generosity
## EXCEED EXPECTATIONS

*Whoever sows sparingly will also reap sparingly,*
*and whoever sows generously will also reap generously.*

—2 Corinthians 9:6

The incredible enthusiasm and exceptional service of a busboy was the spark God used to ignite the SHINE vision in my heart and mind. I was having dinner with some colleagues when, in my opinion, the best busboy in the world began to clear the table next to us. He had focus, a well-thought-out plan, and unparalleled enthusiasm as he flawlessly executed his task. I cannot imagine a time in the history of food service that anyone could more efficiently turn a dirty table into a clean set-up, ready for the next guest. I am not kidding! He was that good.

I could not stop watching this busboy as he worked—putting on the same sparkling demonstration time after time. Others were watching, too, as eventually many diners applauded, right on cue, as he finished setting each table. That night, I could not sleep after witnessing that server at work. The image of the world's greatest busboy would not leave my mind.

But more than that, I found myself wondering if anyone would ever applaud me for the work I do.

Then I began to dream... imagining applause every time I spoke to an employee or served a customer because of the excellent service I had rendered. I envisioned my entire company performing so well that it would glow from the sheer radiance of its own achievements. I reasoned that is what it would look like to shine—to stand out in a way that others would take notice and applaud us for the work we do.

I do not claim to have actually heard God's audible voice. But, at that moment, He spoke directly to my heart. It was time to make some adjustments in my thinking. God revealed that we are indeed called to shine, to stand out in a way that others would take notice. However, He wants us to do so not so that our works would bring us applause, but so the work God does in and through us would inspire others to applaud Him. Here is what Scripture instructs us to do:

> *Arise, shine; for your light has come! And the glory of the Lord is risen upon you. For behold, the darkness shall cover the earth, and deep darkness the people; but the Lord will arise over you, and His glory will be seen upon you.*
>
> —Isaiah 60:1–2, NKJV

## SERVE FROM THE HEART

It amazes me the lengths to which God will go to grab our attention. For Moses, God used a burning bush to get his attention. For the prophet Isaiah, God gave him a vision of the heavenly hosts singing, "Holy, holy, holy is the Lord God almighty." For me, God worked on my heart through the world's greatest busboy.

It does not matter how God gets our attention; He chooses the best means by which to communicate His message to each of us. What is important is the message God imparts to us. When we are in a growing relationship with Him, we continually seek to hear His voice so we love Him more deeply and serve Him out of that love. God desires for each of us to reflect His love to the world and SHINE right where He has placed us. We are to heed His call to serve from the heart for His glory. Martin Luther King, Jr. said it well: "If a man is called to be a street sweeper, he should sweep streets even as Michelangelo painted, or Beethoven composed music, or Shakespeare wrote poetry. He should sweep streets so well that all the hosts of heaven and earth will pause to say, 'Here lived a street sweeper who did his job well.'"

Have you ever received such exceptional service that it was worthy of applause? Ponder for a moment the last time you received outstanding service that completely exceeded your expectations. Often, those instances are difficult to recall. Let me encourage you to pause and think of a time when you received service that exceeded your expectation. What made that service excellent? What was it that exceeded your expectation? How can you apply that experience to your own service to others?

Now think about the last time you received poor service. That should be easier to recall. What was it lacking? Why was your expectation not met? What can you learn from that experience to make sure you deliver better service to others?

I read that the average customer will remember an outstanding service incident for about 18 months but will remember a poor one for about 23.5 years. What a disparity! From that perspective, can you see the value of providing generous service that exceeds expectations?

The fact is, most service we receive meets only our lowest level of expectations. It is average. Rarely do people remember average service. Average service never receives applause.

. . . . . . . . . . . . . . . . . . . . . . . . . . . . . . . . . . . . . . . . . .

*We can give our best effort when we realize we work for God, not for man.*

. . . . . . . . . . . . . . . . . . . . . . . . . . . . . . . . . . . . . . . . . .

The opportunity to provide outstanding service is not tied to position or circumstance. From the top to the bottom of an organization chart, anyone can provide service that shines if they strive to do so. Generosity is reflected by giving our all from the depths of our hearts. We can give our best effort when we realize we work for God, not for man.

> *Whatever you do, work at it with all your heart, as working for the Lord, not for men.*
>
> —Colossians 3:23

The self-serving employee who just wants to get by will seldom be valued very highly in any organization. However, an employee who serves generously increases his or her own value, brings value to others, and honors God in the process.

The choice is yours. Let me encourage you to go ahead and make an impact. Do more than you are paid to do. Give more than what is required. Aim higher than what is expected. Serve with all your heart. Most importantly, do it for Lord.

# SERVE UNCONDITIONALLY

Serving generously requires that we take the initiative to serve. We cannot sit around hoping that opportunity will come and find us. Waiting for a better time doesn't work. Instead, we should intentionally seek opportunities to serve. This approach is good for us, good for others, and good for business. Proactively initiating service without requirement is the first step toward exceeding expectations.

Generous service is not selective service. Someone's position, station in life, or relative importance should not matter. Along those lines, it is easy to serve people we know and like, but much harder to serve those we do not. Likewise, it is easy to serve when we anticipate a reward and not so easy when we see no obvious personal benefit. Yet if we are to serve generously, we should be willing to serve anyone without making arbitrary judgments.

My dad tells a story that illustrates this well. It had been a long week, and he was ready to head home to the family. On his way to his car, he met a middle-aged gentleman wearing grungy clothes and driving a beat-up truck. The fellow said he wanted to look at a tree-transplanting machine for a local project. Based on this man's appearance, my dad assumed this would be a waste of time. However, he took the man into the equipment yard and rushed through a presentation. The fellow seemed impressed. He told my dad he would arrange to buy a machine on Monday.

"I'll never see that guy again," my dad thought as he drove home that night. And he was right. He never did see the same person again. However, the first thing on Monday morning, he did see a property manager, who brought him a check for a new tree-transplanting machine. In a conversation with the property manager, my dad came to realize that the gentleman whom he had helped on Friday night was Kemmons Wilson, the founder of the Holiday Inn hotel chain.

Generous service pays no attention to perceived status. A great way to think about this is to remember that we will never meet anybody who does not matter to God. He cares for us all.

*Live in harmony with each other. Don't be too proud to enjoy the company of ordinary people...Do things in such a way that everyone can see you are honorable.*

—Romans 12:16–17, NLT

# GO THE EXTRA MILE

When Jesus walked the earth, His people were governed by Roman law. During this period of history, Roman soldiers could demand that a Jewish citizen drop what he or she was doing and serve them, by carrying their equipment for one mile, at any time. It was the law. Understandably, this law was not popular among the people. They saw it as one more visible sign of their oppression under Roman rule.

Jesus, however, took a totally different perspective. Instead of complaining, He exhorted His followers to do more than what the law required: "If someone forces you to go one mile, go with him two miles" (Matt. 5:41). In other words, always exceed expectations.

Too often today, we view our work as just another sign of our own oppression. That is why some people quickly establish the lowest acceptable standards for performing their jobs—doing just enough to squeeze by. For example, many of us have thought or said statements like these:

*"It's the same old job, just a different day."*

*"It's not my problem; someone else is to blame."*

*"They don't pay me enough to do that."*

*"It's not my job; let someone else do it."*

*"Nobody even appreciates what I do."*

*"I can't believe they expect that of me."*

These statements all describe first-mile thinking. They come from the depths of self-pity and reveal a hapless "I'm oppressed" mindset. Jesus calls us to go beyond the minimum standards. He calls us to rise above the attitude of oppression, to stop worrying about what's fair, and to focus on what is right. The first mile is focused on self and what we must do to survive in our work. The second mile is focused on going above and beyond expectations to serve generously. It is on the second mile that we shine at work. Second-mile statements are more like these:

*"This is a great opportunity to serve."*

*"I'm sorry that happened to you. How can I help?"*

*"Thank you for this opportunity. I appreciate it very much."*

*"I will do my best to serve your need."*

*"What else can I do for you?"*

*"How can I serve you better in the future?"*

# EXCEED EXPECTATIONS

Opportunities to serve often come to us disguised as problems. If someone comes to you and presents a problem, be careful not to deflect your opportunity to serve. Do not blame someone else, and don't make excuses for the problem. Regardless of who or what caused the problem, look for creative ways to solve it. Take responsibility, regardless of where the blame lies. When we respond in this manner, problems become opportunities to SHINE.

Generous service begins by understanding the situation, taking responsibility, and then reacting in a positive manner.

In the book *The Generosity Factor*, author Kenneth Blanchard and Chick-fil-A founder S. Truett Cathy, write, "A lot of folks say they care about people, but they don't actually do anything about it. Generosity is all about caring about the needs of others, then acting to meet those needs…about balance… about making all of one's resources available."[1]

· · · · · · · · · · · · · · · · · · · · · · · · · · · · · · · · · · · · · · · ·

*We serve because God calls us to serve.*

· · · · · · · · · · · · · · · · · · · · · · · · · · · · · · · · · · · · · · · ·

In business, companies that serve generously tend to also reap generously. Employees who serve generously will make the biggest impact. Yet it is helpful to understand the difference between serving generously and pleasing others.

---

1. Kenneth H. Blanchard and S. Truett Cathy, *The Generosity Factor* (Grand Rapids, MI: Zondervan, 2002), 43.

Serving generously does not mean trying to make everyone happy. We can get distracted and disappointed if pleasing others becomes our goal. The truth is, we will never make everyone happy with our service. We cannot control someone else's happiness, but we *can* control how and why we serve. We do not serve others just to please them; we serve others because God has called us to serve. Serving with generosity means giving our best for the glory of God in all circumstances. Therefore, our goal is not to please people but to serve as God has instructed.

> *So whether you eat or drink or whatever you do, do it all for the glory of God.*
> —1 Corinthians 10:31

A helpful practice is to visualize God watching our every move as we carry out our duties. That should kick up our enthusiasm a bit. As followers of Christ, we should be serving Him with generosity, regardless of our personal circumstance or status. In doing so, we are putting more into life than we are taking out. We are modeling Christ-like behavior for the world to the glory of God. We serve others through uncommon generosity.

Exceed expectations!

# SERVE OTHERS

Humility—Put Others First

Compassion—Show You Care

Generosity—Exceed Expectations

*A heart of servanthood glorifies God*

*by helping others.*

PRINCIPLE TWO

# HONOR GOD

*But seek first His Kingdom and His righteousness,*
*and all these things will be given to you as well.*

—MATTHEW 6:33

## CHAPTER 5

# Ignite the Flame of Faithfulness
## A SOUL OF FAITHFULNESS OBEYS GOD'S PURPOSE

*Let love and faithfulness never leave you; bind them around your neck, write them on the tablet of your heart.*

—Proverbs 3:3

The first edition of this book, *SHINE*, was released in January 2008. Although much has transpired since then, the most compelling and life-transforming event of my life occurred later that year.

It was Christmas time. With a business to lead and three young children at home, our lives did not lack activity. Add to that a cold virus that had worked its way through our family. We eventually felt better, except for my nine-year-old daughter, Gracyn. She was prescribed an antibiotic and breathing treatment. Yet, she could not seem to shake it. By Christmas Eve morning, she could not muster the strength to climb out of bed. I carried her to the car so my wife, Robin, could rush her to see the doctor. Next, a frantic call came from Robin: "We are in an ambulance speeding to the hospital. Can you get there immediately?"

It was there we learned a virus had settled into Gracyn's heart. The diagnosis: a condition called *viral myocarditis*. One-third of people can heal from it, one-third will need a heart transplant, and one-third will die from it. We were shocked. Immediately, we began to pray fervently that Gracyn would be in the optimal one-third. However, it was not to be. By later that night, she would be sustained by full life-support equipment. As they were putting her on a breathing machine, she screamed out, "I'm going to die!" Those were the last words we heard from her that night.

I will never forget that Christmas morning. Sustained by machines, our daughter was barely clinging to life. The doctor told us there was nothing they could do for her. It was in this moment—the one I, as a parent, had feared beyond any other—Robin and I received the greatest Christmas gift ever. In the most chaotic event of our lives, there was peace, the kind of peace only God can give.

*Be still and know I am God.* —Psalm 46:10

What Robin heard when the doctor delivered this news is, Gracyn is not in the doctor's hands anymore. She is in God's hands. What I heard is, Only God can do this. Robin and I hugged, cried, and prayed as we placed our only daughter in the hands of the One who created her. We knew if God kept her in heaven, she would be healed there. We could accept that if it was God's will. Yet we kept praying for a miracle that would allow her to return to us.

The next few days are a blur. Eventually, they informed us that the machines could not keep Gracyn alive much longer. I sat quietly as I watched Robin exemplify one of the greatest moments of faith I had ever observed. "Gracyn is in God's hands now," she said. "We know that no matter what happens, our daughter is going to be okay."

Not long afterward, the head of cardiology informed us of an experimental machine called a Berlin heart that could potentially keep Gracyn alive longer. It was not yet approved by the FDA; however, a doctor at the University of Florida had performed three of these experimental care surgeries. Upon praying, we still felt a peace that surpassed all understanding. So we allowed Gracyn to become a case study in a medical experiment. She was airlifted one hundred miles north to Shands Hospital at the University of Florida. There we embarked on an ongoing journey of faith on which I will expand in the opening of the upcoming chapters of this section.

I tell you this story to make this point: we honor God when we remain faithful to Him in all circumstances. While it is great to honor God from the mountaintop, what about when we are walking through the darkest of valleys? Eventually, we all face crucibles in our lives. *Crucibles* are those moments of truth when our innermost beliefs are put to the ultimate test.

- Does our faith fade away, or does it become our sight?
- Do we rely on self, or do we trust God with the outcome?
- Do we turn from God and blame Him, or do we turn to God, thankful that He controls all things?

## FAITHFUL PEOPLE

Faithfulness is one of the most important qualities a person can possess. I hate to think where I would be were it not for my faith in Jesus Christ. Yet faithfulness is a character quality not often linked to the workplace. When the term *faithful* is used at work, it is often misunderstood.

For many years, I traveled to our various locations to discuss employee performance with our local managers. I loved hearing how people were doing and discussing how we could help them improve. Once, an operations manager referred to a certain employee as an underperformer with a negative attitude. This manager went on to explain that he had done everything possible to help this employee succeed. Yet he had seen no improvement. The next statement really floored me: "But he is probably one of the most faithful employees I have ever had." To this manager, faithfulness meant that one had been around a while and always showed up for work. Obviously, faithfulness requires much more than that. As a side note, both this employee and his manager have since moved on to seek other opportunities.

It is true: showing up every day is a good idea. A faithful employee, however, should also be trustworthy and reliable—someone who can be counted on to get the job done right. Faithful employees are loyal, dependable, dedicated, and committed to giving their best effort, regardless of circumstance. They do the right things for the right reasons. Faithful employees positively impact an organization through their positive example.

At the same time, faithful employers should be fair and just and care deeply for the employees of an organization. They should always deliver what they promise. Faithful employers are committed to high standards of performance, help employees improve, and cultivate a culture of honesty and ethical morality. Faithful employers do not tolerate behavior that contradicts the values and culture of the organization. They commit to correcting unsatisfactory behavior and, ultimately, to improving or removing it from the organization. Faithfulness requires strict adherence to the principles and values to which the leaders of an organization believe are most important.

# FAITHFUL PROVIDER

Faithfulness is used often in the Bible as a description of God. God's faithfulness is mentioned more than thirty times alone in the book of Psalms. Every aspect of a believer's life is anchored in the faithfulness of a God who has never failed us.

> *Your Kingdom is an everlasting kingdom, and your dominion endures through all generations. The Lord is faithful to all His promises and loving toward all He has made.*
>
> —Psalm 145:13

So, to whom should we pledge our faithfulness? Is it our boss, our company, the code of ethics, the board of directors? Sometimes employers do not even stand for the ideals we value. Sometimes we may view our work as insignificant and not worthy of faithfulness. These are only some of the reasons that faithfulness is not all that common in the workplace.

Scripture tells us, *"If you are faithful in little things, you will be faithful in large ones… "* (Luke 16:10, NLT). Regardless of who our boss is, where we work, or what job we hold, God still desires faithfulness in all we do. He continually develops our faithfulness in the small things so He can use our faithfulness in much more important things.

. . . . . . . . . . . . . . . . . . . . . . . . . . . . . . . . . . . . . . . . . . . .

*God isn't looking for people*

*who just show up.*

. . . . . . . . . . . . . . . . . . . . . . . . . . . . . . . . . . . . . . . . . . . .

Family counselor and best-selling author John Trent said, "Imagine getting up in the morning not dreading but dedicated to going to work for a purpose—His purpose for you in your workplace! You may never change the entire corporate culture where you work, but you can change lives—your own and many others as well."[1]

God is not looking for people who just show up. He is looking for those He can count on to build His Kingdom. He wants us to trust Him in all we do. God is faithful to provide for all the needs of those who follow Him.

*My eyes will be on the faithful in the land that they may dwell with Me...*

—Psalm 101:6

# FAITHFUL POWER

If you are like me, you probably question how your work could possibly honor and glorify God. I spent years struggling with this concept. Eventually, I asked in prayer, "What do You want from me, God? I'm only an equipment salesman. I'm not qualified to build your Kingdom. How could I possibly honor You with the work I do?"

At that point, God began to reveal an astonishing truth to me: He does not call the equipped to do His work. He equips those whom He calls so He can work through them. It does not matter how qualified we are, what we do for a living, or where we live. What matters is our calling to love Him, obey Him, and seek Him with heart, soul, mind, and strength. It is through this faithfulness that God works in

---

1. John Trent, quoted in William Nix, *Transforming Your Workplace for Christ* (Nashville, TN: Broadman & Holman Publishers, 1997), xii.

us and reveals Himself: *"For it is God who works in you to will and to act according to His good purpose"* (Phil. 2:13). It is not what we do for God that honors Him. It is what God does through us that brings Him glory.

. . . . . . . . . . . . . . . . . . . . . . . . . . . . . . . . . . . . . . . . . . .

*It Is not what we do for God, but what God does through us that brings Him glory.*

. . . . . . . . . . . . . . . . . . . . . . . . . . . . . . . . . . . . . . . . . . .

It is hard for me to fathom why God would choose to work through ordinary individuals like us to accomplish His purposes. But that is exactly what He does! Throughout time, God has done, and continues to do, extraordinary works through ordinary people who are faithful to Him. Agnes Bojaxhiu, a humble social worker better known as Mother Teresa, said this: "I am nothing. He is all. I do nothing of my own. He does it. I am God's pencil. A tiny bit of pencil with which He writes what He likes. God writes through us, and however imperfect instruments we may be, He writes beautifully."

## FAITHFUL PURPOSE

As we honor our relationship with God, He works in us and carries out His purposes through us. We do not have to be a pastor, a missionary, or the president of a company to honor Him with our work. The Bible calls all believers *a royal priesthood* (see 1 Peter

2:9). Regardless of our profession or position, we are all called to ministry. We honor God by making our relationship with Him our top priority. It is His faithfulness that inspires our hearts and souls, guides our thoughts and emotions, and leads us to faithfully pursue these godly purposes:

- Love God.
- Reflect God's glory.
- Provide for needs.
- Build God's Kingdom.

..............................................

## *A soul of faithfulness obeys God's purpose.*

..............................................

Faithfulness is not a quality we can build on our own. It is rather a natural response to seeing, believing, and experiencing God's faithfulness at work in our lives. Faithful lives honor God by revealing trust in Him, through gratitude glorifying Him, and by stewardship meeting needs as He builds His Kingdom through us. A soul of faithfulness obeys God's purpose. Scripture reminds us that God's master purpose will always be accomplished.

*Many are the plans in a man's heart, but it is the Lord's purpose that prevails.*

—Proverbs 19:21

## CHAPTER 6

# Shine with Trust

## DEPEND ON HIM

*Trust in the Lord with all your heart and lean not on your own understanding; in all your ways acknowledge Him, and He will make your paths straight.*

—Proverbs 3:5–6

Still in a coma and on full life-support equipment, Gracyn flew with her Orlando care team by helicopter to Gainesville, Florida. We drove by car to join her at UF Health Shands Hospital. Immediately upon our arrival there, we began to experience doubt. This was all new. We did not know anybody there. We were not home anymore. Exhaustion was taking its toll. At times, we could not think straight. Yet we knew our daughter's survival and our ability to cope with it would require that our trust in God rise to a level beyond our reach.

Anxiety was high as we met her new care team. They explained that her condition was worse than expected. The lead surgeon assured us they would use every means possible to save her life. The more they spoke, the more I could feel God easing my mind. I knew God was in control, and He would use this team to care for my daughter. Robin agreed. The only thing we could do was trust God, no matter what might happen.

The surgery to implant the Berlin heart—the experimental device that would substitute for my daughter's failed heart—went well. We learned that while on life support, her vital organs were close to shutting down, and she had suffered a stroke that could lead to brain damage. Robin again assured our new caregivers that Gracyn was in God's hands and she would be fine. Her faith inspired me and everyone else around us.

As time ticked by, we realized we had been given a front-row seat to experience God's miraculous grace and healing power. Gracyn's steady improvement shocked her caregivers. Soon Gracyn was coming out of her coma and moving her hands and legs upon request. As they removed the breathing tube, she tried to talk but could not. One sign of brain damage would be the inability to talk. The care team reassured us that her lungs were full of fluid, and she would not be able to talk immediately due to that. It had been more than a week since my little girl had fearfully screamed those heartbreaking words, "I'm going to die." Her next words were even more incredible. As she squeezed my hand, she whispered in a barely audible voice, "Daddy, I love you." From *I'm going to die* to *Daddy, I love you*: what a miracle!

I would like to say it was a smooth road from that point forward; however, nothing could be further from the truth. For months, we would face seemingly insurmountable challenges. Yet we took on each trial with confidence as we trusted God each step of the way.

## GODLY TRUST

Obviously, this extraordinary situation required extreme trust. I had never faced such a dire predicament before or since. Some may never face a scenario like this. Yet in less dramatic ways, we all face situations in our daily lives that require a choice of where we place our trust.

At work, it is easy to place our trust in the wrong things. If not careful, we can find ourselves trusting in money, power, position, and sometimes the wrong people. We put pressure on ourselves to advance, stand out, and strive for success. Yet, more important than reaching these goals is how we choose to get there. Do we trust in our own power, or do we trust in God? The author of Proverbs wrote, *"Commit to the Lord whatever you do, and your plans will succeed"* (Prov. 16:3). Our personal and professional goals should be focused on doing life and work God's way by trusting in His plan and relying on His power.

Still, I often choose to trust in my own strength rather than in God's power. In our company, nearly two hundred employees are counting on me and trusting in my leadership to guide us to enduring success. At times, this responsibility energizes me, and at other times, the stress takes its toll. One day, I was agonizing over a situation, and one of our managers walked in and shut the door behind him. "Something's weighing on you, Kris," he said. "How can I help?"

"I wish you could," I told him. "But there really is nothing you can do." I mustered as much bravado as possible and tried to assure him he need not worry. "As the leader of this company, I need to deal with this situation myself."

We chatted a bit longer, and then he got up to walk out of the room. However, before he left, he caught my eye and said, "You are confident in God, and for that reason alone, I am confident in you. I trust you because I know you trust Him."

This manager reminded me that the confidence others place in me is directly related to the confidence I—and they—place in God. When we trust in Him, it relieves the stress we place on ourselves. We honor God by placing our confident hope in Him to provide the best outcome.

> *Those who hope in the Lord will renew their strength. They will soar on wings like eagles.*
>
> —Isaiah 40:31

# EARNED TRUST

Trust is the foundation of successful relationships. It is also the foundation of successful organizations. Trust is not an entitlement but a virtue that is established over time. Our actions continually are evaluated by those with whom we interact to determine our level of trustworthiness. As trust grows, opportunity and responsibility also grow with it.

A primary role of leadership is to develop a high level of trust within the organization. Accordingly, the enduring success of an organization is built on the trustworthiness of its leaders. Likewise, trusted employees are most likely to receive promotions and greater opportunity. Customers strongly desire to do business with people they trust.

I once had a notoriously demanding customer call to discuss his feelings about one of our service managers. He said, "Nobody makes me angrier than your service manager. He never tells me what I want to hear. He never budges to any of my demands. But he always comes through with what he promises. Most people tell me what I want to hear and then let me down. But not him—he has earned my trust.

That's why I keep coming back."

A great way to earn trust is to do the following:

1. Do what you say.

2. Do it when you say you'll do it.

3. Do it right the first time.

4. Always under-promise and over-deliver.

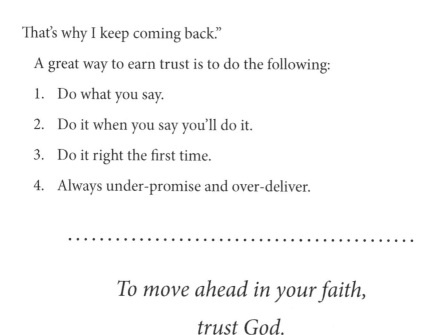

*To move ahead in your faith,*

*trust God.*

Once trust is earned, loyalty results. One of the greatest compliments anyone can receive is in hearing the words, "I trust you." Similarly, we express our love for God through actions that reveal our trust in Him. God blesses those who trust Him. In fact, the more we trust in God, the more He entrusts to us: *"Now it is required that those who have been given a trust must prove faithful"* (1 Corin. 4:2). The more we step out in trusting obedience, the more faithful we become and the more loyal we are proven.

## OBEDIENT TRUST

If you want to move ahead in your work, be a person worthy of trust. If you want to move ahead in your faith, simply trust God. The key to establishing and maintaining trust is found in obedience to God and His will. Trust and obedience go hand in hand. Trust confirms our internal beliefs. Obedience reveals this faith through the external behavior evidenced in our works.

In *Experiencing God,* author and renowned Bible teacher Henry Blackaby compares a self-centered life to a God-centered life:[1]

| Self-Centered | God-Centered |
|---|---|
| Life focused on self | Life focused on God |
| Pride in self and self's own accomplishments | Humility before God |
| Self-confidence | Confidence in God |
| Depending on self and self's own abilities | Dependence on God, His ability and provision |
| Affirming self | Denying self |
| Seeking to be acceptable to the world and its ways | Seeking first the Kingdom of God and His righteousness |
| Looking at circumstances from a human perspective | Seeking God's perspective in every circumstance |
| Selfish and ordinary living | Holy and godly living |

How would you describe your life at work? Is it self-centered, or is it God-centered? When our lives reveal trust in and obedience to Him, we become available for God to work in us to accomplish His purposes for His glory.

---

1. Henry Blackaby and Claude V. King, *Experiencing God* (Nashville, TN: Broadman & Holman, 1994), 100–101.

# RELIANT TRUST

We demonstrate our trust in God when we bow to Him in prayer. Never are we more in touch with God's power than when we are on our knees in prayer.

*I lift up my eyes to the hills—where does my help come from? My help comes from the Lord, the Maker of heaven and earth.*

—Psalm 121:1–2

I used to pray for specific outcomes for our business. I would think about what I wanted, and then I would pray that God would provide it. I have come to learn that this is a very limiting and selfish type of prayer. The outcomes we desire pale in comparison to God's plans.

Years ago, one of our top sales reps, Mark, was offered a sales manager position by another company. I feared the thought of losing Mark because I knew he had great potential. As I began to pray that God would make him stay, it became clear that my prayer was inappropriate. Instead, I needed to trust in God to provide for our company and pray for God's will to be done for Mark and his future.

Mark agonized for weeks over this tough decision. It was difficult for me to refrain from persuading him to stay. One afternoon on the phone, I suggested that only God knew what this decision should be, and I asked Mark if I could pray for him. He said it was okay, so I prayed, "God, you are in control of all aspects of our lives. You are in control of this difficult decision. I trust you will make your way known to Mark. Let your will be done on earth as it is in heaven."

The next morning, Mark informed me that he would be leaving our company. While thanking him for his service, a strong leading overcame me to discuss salvation with him. As uncomfortable as the timing was, I blurted out, "I'm not nearly as concerned about where you spend the next few years working as about where you will spend eternity." I explained my trust in Jesus, my belief in eternal life, and my desire to see Mark in heaven one day. He grew increasingly uncomfortable. Suddenly, Mark jumped up, said, "I have to go" and swiftly left my office.

A few days later, he called to inform me about his change of heart. Mark explained that his mother had been praying for him to find Jesus. She had mentioned to her pastor the difficult work decision her son was facing. The pastor committed to pray. A few days later, the pastor had called and said, "I really think your son needs to stay where he is. I feel he is where God wants him to be." This pastor was more than thirteen hundred miles away and knew little about our company. He just felt led to share this counsel because he had been praying for God's guidance in this situation.

I am extremely pleased that Mark stayed with our company, and he has since grown into one of the top leaders in our organization. More importantly, God used that time in his life to bring Mark into a relationship with Jesus.

· · · · · · · · · · · · · · · · · · · · · · · · · · · · · · · · · · · · · · · ·

*Honor God with trust.*

*Depend on Him.*

· · · · · · · · · · · · · · · · · · · · · · · · · · · · · · · · · · · · · · · ·

Sometimes the greatest thing we can do for someone is simply to lift their name in prayer. It continues to amaze me what God does when we trust Him and leave the outcome to Him. When we trust God, He removes the stress we place on ourselves. We no longer place our trust in money, power, people, or other resources. Instead, we trust in almighty God, the provider of all resources and relationships. By trusting God, we, too, become trustworthy.

## CHAPTER 7

# Shine with Gratitude

## THANK HIM

*We should be grateful that we were given a kingdom that cannot be shaken. And in this kingdom we please God by worshiping Him and by showing Him great honor and respect.*

— Hebrews 12:28, CEV

As Gracyn steadily recovered from her coma, it was clear she had spent time with the Lord. She was quoting Scripture and telling us that Jesus was healing her. When she met her surgeon, she asked him for a hug. As he reached down to oblige, Gracyn told him, "Thank you for saving my life. God is doing miracles, and He is using you to do them." He was moved to tears. There is not a person on this earth I am more grateful for than Mark Bleiweis, the surgeon whose hands God used to save Gracyn's life.

Over time, Gracyn began to understand she was stuck in a hospital. The Berlin heart requires tubes embedded under the rib cage that connect to an artery and the heart. Blood is pumped through these tubes, out of the body to the machine, and then returned to the heart. The Berlin heart mimics the function of a human heart and can sustain patients for months as they wait on a heart for transplant. It is an amazing yet brutal sight. Gracyn was in constant pain and discomfort. Our hearts would melt each time she cried out. Worse than the pain was her not knowing if or when she would ever get to go home. It was excruciating. Every day was a physical, spiritual, and emotional battle. Some days presented life-and-death situations. Other days included simple struggles like going to the bathroom or taking medications while constantly hooked to a machine. Tough stuff for anyone, let alone a nine-year-old who had always been healthy.

Robin and I rented an apartment near the hospital to be close. Each day, one or both of us stayed with Gracyn. The toughest thing to do at night was to leave her alone so we could go get some sleep. Every morning, we would awaken to the shattering disappointment this was not just a dream but our reality. Robin and I agreed we needed to be strong and positive around Gracyn. We also committed to always show gratitude to our Lord. A small action that helped was to think about thanking God for things we were grateful for each morning. This gave us the strength to face the coming day.

We always thanked her caregivers and encouraged Gracyn to do the same. Robin would walk through the intensive care unit singing songs of praise to Jesus. Everyone knew she was the mom whose daughter was hooked to an experimental machine. Praise and gratitude can be trusty guides as we navigate through the storms that come our way.

## GRATEFUL THOUGHTS

It all starts with how we look at things. Many people view work as a game or a battlefield—striving to win and jockeying for advancement. From this viewpoint, pride and ego are built around personal achievement and making more money. To some, work is a curse, a rat race, or just a necessary evil. Seldom do we hear work described as a blessing.

Often, we are more apt to brag about personal accomplishments or grumble about work than we are to express gratitude and thankfulness for it. Sometimes we can get so wrapped up in self and in trying to get ahead that we forget the importance of having and expressing gratitude. Bragging about achievements or complaining about our work fosters ungrateful thoughts and moves us away from faithfulness. On the other hand, thankfulness yields grateful thoughts and can increase our faithfulness.

In 1 Thessalonians 5:16–18, we are instructed, *"Be joyful always; pray continually; give thanks in all circumstances, for this is God's will for you in Christ Jesus."* From this viewpoint, gratitude is expressed in all we do. Our work, indeed, is a blessing from God, which provides for our needs, gives us something productive to do, and allows us to positively impact others as we carry out the purposes for which we were created.

# GRATEFUL ATTITUDES

Unfortunately, work is often overlooked when it comes to expressing our gratitude. We may regularly give thanks for a nice day, our houses, or the food we eat. But how often do we express gratitude for our work? We may not feel grateful because we feel underappreciated, overworked, or underutilized.

There are numerous reasons for frustration, disappointment, and thanklessness at work. However, when this happens, we should rethink our circumstances and our attitude. Nothing more quickly diminishes our work life than an ungrateful attitude. Conversely, nothing more quickly improves our work life than a thankful and grateful mind-set.

If you would like to improve your attitude at work, here is something to try. When you arrive at work, take a moment to thank God for providing you with the blessing of work. Think of three things you are thankful for regarding your work, and thank the Lord for them. When we fill our minds with thankful thoughts and prayers, it prepares our hearts for grateful service that honors God. When our hearts are filled with gratitude, our words and actions will reflect praise and thankfulness in all circumstances.

*But giving thanks is a sacrifice that truly honors me. If you keep to my path, I will reveal to you the salvation of God.*
—Psalm 50:23, NLT

. . . . . . . . . . . . . . . . . . . . . . . . . . . . . . . . . . . . . . .

## *God provides work as a blessing.*

. . . . . . . . . . . . . . . . . . . . . . . . . . . . . . . . . . . . . . .

We have all encountered people who arrogantly take credit for their success without thanking those who helped them along the way. Often, these individuals are insecure and unhappy. On the other hand, those we meet who are grateful and willing to praise others usually have a propensity to lead more joyful lives. Business owners, leaders, and highly successful professionals always should be among the most grateful. An appreciative boss who regularly thanks God, employees, customers, and others sets a standard of gratitude for the entire organization. It is of great importance for leaders to be keenly aware of the influence their gratitude will have on those around them.

As an employee, regardless of your boss's level of gratitude, you are responsible for your own attitude of thankfulness. Do not be negatively influenced by others. Set your own tone of grateful appreciation. Sincere appreciation goes a long way. People love to hear the words "Thank you." By thanking others, you pass on your gratitude and encourage them with your uplifting attitude of appreciation.

Thanking God and others tends to multiply our blessings. Gratitude is an endearing quality that not only lifts our own spirits but also lifts the spirits of those around us. Once our attitude of gratitude has reached the heart level, people will begin to see a difference. When we are grateful for our work, we find more enjoyment, fulfillment, and satisfaction in all we do.

*So I saw that there is nothing better for people than to be happy in their work. That is why we are here...*

—Ecclesiastes 3:22, NLT

# GRATEFUL WORSHIP

Worship. It is a basic need of all humans. Although not everyone chooses to worship Jesus, we are all wired for worship. Just as the body needs food to survive, our souls are fed by worship. With that in mind, have you ever considered your work as an opportunity to worship God? Not many people think that way. In fact, many people are more likely to worship their work than they are to see their work as an opportunity to worship God. But it does not have to be that way.

Work was mandated—and blessed—by God at creation: *"The Lord God took the man and put him in the Garden of Eden to work it and take care of it"* (Gen. 2:15). In this Scripture passage, the original Hebrew word translated "to work" is *a'vodah*. The word *a'vodah* has dual meanings: it can be translated to mean both work and worship. Therefore, work could be considered the original form of worship. Before there was a church, a song, a creed, or any other form of worship, there was a workplace: the Garden. Adam worshipped God by caring for His creation. Adam's work, indeed, was an expression of his worship. So is ours.

. . . . . . . . . . . . . . . . . . . . . . . . . . . . . . . . . . . . . . . . . .

## *God is praised by committed hearts.*

. . . . . . . . . . . . . . . . . . . . . . . . . . . . . . . . . . . . . . . . . .

Pastor and best-selling author Rick Warren wrote, "Worship is a lifestyle of enjoying God, loving Him, and giving ourselves to be used for His purposes. When you use your life for God's glory, everything you do can become an act of worship."[1]

Far too often, we try to compartmentalize our worship by thinking worship is what we do at church on Sunday and work is what we do the rest of the week. I am quite sure God does not view it that way. As we more fully understand that God is praised not as much by our raised hands on Sunday morning as He is by committed hearts throughout the week, our whole perspective of worship can begin

1. Rick Warren, *The Purpose Driven Life* (Grand Rapids, MI: Zondervan, 2002), 56.

to change. Worship and work become one and the same when we commit our efforts to the glory of God.

> *So let the peace that comes from Christ control your thoughts. And be grateful. Whatever you say or do should be done in the name of the Lord Jesus, as you give thanks to God the Father because of Him.*
> —Colossians 3:15,17, CEV

# GRATEFUL PRAISE

Worship may seem distant while we are under the stress of completing a project, dealing with an employee issue, taking care of a disgruntled customer, or facing household responsibilities. We can easily become distracted by the challenges at hand. When this occurs, a simple prayer of gratitude offered up in the midst of our busyness can help align our hearts with worship and fortify our souls. When things get hectic, we can find great peace in taking a moment for a quick spiritual retreat right where we are. A simple prayer of gratitude can lift us in the midst of tumultuous surroundings:

> *Jesus, You are Lord. Thank you for loving me. Thank you for living in me. Empower me through your Spirit. Praise be to God. Amen.*

Through thanksgiving and praise, we reveal faithfulness:

> *Enter His gates with thanksgiving and His courts with praise; give thanks to Him and praise His name. For the Lord is good and His love endures forever; His faithfulness continues through all generations.*
> —Psalm 100:4–5

Thank God for providing the blessing of work! Let our good works praise His Name. We thank God for what He does, and we praise

Him for who He is. He alone is worthy of our worship and heartfelt gratitude. We all have so much for which to be grateful.

A thankful heart tunes us into God's wonder and opens us up to His blessings. Through thanksgiving and praise, we demonstrate our gratitude to God as we love Him with heart and soul.

## CHAPTER 8

# Shine with Stewardship

## SERVE HIM

*What are mere mortals that you should think about them,*

*human beings that you should care for them? …You gave them charge*

*of everything you made, putting all things under their authority*

—Psalm 8:4,6 NLT

With Easter quickly approaching, Gracyn was growing all the more weary. This was her fourth month in intensive care waiting for a heart that may never come. I wrote this on the care page we used to keep people up to date:

*As I watch Gracyn drift to sleep, I can't explain the pain I feel as her father. Oh, if I could just trade places with her. But I can't. Her arms are covered in bruises from the countless shots she receives daily. Of course, you can't miss the tubes embedded in her body that provide the lifeline from the artificial heart to her arteries. It's hard to imagine four months ago she was fully healthy. Tonight I find myself wondering how much more can she endure. Will this ever end?*

*As the pain of fatherhood reaches the depths of my soul, it is here that I find refuge. I am comforted in knowing my Father in heaven understands this pain. He watched His own Son endure much more so that you and I might call Him Savior. It's reassuring to know we can call upon a God who knows our pain and that He alone has a plan to overcome it.*

. . . . . . . . . . . . . . . . . . . . . . . . . . . . . . . . . . . . . . .

*Lord, You know I'm waiting.*

*I wait in faith…acknowledging You are in control.*

*I wait in confidence…knowing You are almighty.*

*I wait in gratitude…for what you are going to do.*

*I wait in dependence…knowing You are all I need.*

*And I wait in stillness…knowing You are my God.*

. . . . . . . . . . . . . . . . . . . . . . . . . . . . . . . . . . . . . . .

On April 15th, our excruciating wait came to a conclusion. They finally found a match: a new heart for Gracyn. As she entered the operating room, she prayed this prayer:

*Dear God, thank you that you may have sent a new heart for me. I pray that it will heal me. But I want you to know if it doesn't work out the way I want it to, I'm still going to trust you.*

Oh, the pure faith of a child—the type of faith God uses to move our mountains. That night, Gracyn received the perfect heart. Since then, she has thrived. At the time of this writing, Gracyn has returned to the University of Florida—this time as a college student at the very place she endured such pain leading to the gift of a lifetime. Many lessons were learned on this journey; however, none is more important than knowing that God is the Creator and Sustainer of all things. We do not fully comprehend that Jesus is all we need until we realize that Jesus is all we've got. We honor God by faithfully trusting Him, thanking Him, and seeking to be good stewards of all that He entrusts to us.

# PERSPECTIVE OF STEWARDSHIP

An essential truth we learned on this journey is that children are gifts from the Lord. They are our responsibility for a time, yet they always remain His. As parents, we are to be faithful stewards of God's children. We are to take the perspective that God owns every person and everything. He is the owner. We are His stewards.

Simply stated, a *steward* is a manager of someone else's belongings. Good stewards take great care of all with which they have been entrusted. Personally, I had always considered stewardship as strictly a monetary thing. I thought I was a pretty good steward due to my conservative financial management and consistent tithing. Funding God's work through tithing (generally considered as a percentage of our income) and giving (any freewill gift beyond a tithe) is indeed a valid display of obedience.

But faithful stewardship involves much more than just giving money to good causes.

Stewardship is an expression of how we choose to live out our lives and how we spend our time. For instance, we are each given 168 hours per week. How many of those hours are lived devoted to God and to His purposes? Do we pour it all into a single hour of putting on our Sunday best, or do we shine all week in time spent with family, with neighbors, and in the workplace? Gathering for formal worship is significant for nourishing our souls. However, true stewardship is revealed through the other 167 hours of living each week.

Faithful stewardship requires a shift in our perspective of ownership. A steward understands that all things are God's. He owns it all, and He has entrusted us to care for His resources. We are merely stewards of the blessings He provides. From this viewpoint, stewardship frees us to share from 100 percent of our blessings rather than from a small percentage of our income. Once we understand that all things belong to God, it is then that true stewardship begins.

For example, although I am the majority shareholder of our organization, God owns our company. He is the real boss. He has entrusted time, knowledge, resources, and relationships to my care. In various ways and means, God entrusts each of us with work and resources. He calls us to honor Him with faithful stewardship in all we do.

# PRIORITY OF STEWARDSHIP

Without proper stewardship, it is easy to get our priorities skewed when it comes to our work. For many, the purpose of work is to make a lot of money to pursue the lifestyle they desire. However, a steward realizes that a priority on personal riches leads to eventual loss, whereas a priority on God brings eternal blessings: *"A faithful man will be richly blessed, but one eager to get rich will not go unpunished"* (Prov. 28:20).

There is nothing wrong with building wealth and making money. Many godly people are wealthy. But financial status is not what God measures. He looks deeply into our souls and measures our devotion to Him. Our priorities—where we spend our time and resources—reveal where our true devotion lies: *"Where your treasure is, there your heart will be also"* (Matt. 6:21).

God calls us to a loving relationship where Christ is Lord. That means our lives belong fully to Him. As faithful stewards, we should allow Him to govern every penny we spend, every moment of our time, every thought that runs through our minds, every relationship we encounter, every action we take. It is all His. We are simply stewards of whatever God gives us. When He is our priority, then He alone provides our purpose in life and in work.

> *If we live, it's to honor the Lord. And if we die, it's to honor the Lord. So whether we live or die, we belong to the Lord. Christ died and rose again for this very purpose—to be Lord both of the living and of the dead.*
>
> —Romans 14:8–9, NLT

When He is Lord, we no longer are driven by making money, impressing others, or building our own kingdoms. We prioritize honoring Him simply by loving Him from the depths of our soul. When we honor God with faithful stewardship, everything else falls into place.

# PROVISION OF STEWARDSHIP

God uses our work to meet physical needs for food, clothing, shelter, health care, education, et cetera. He can also use our work to meet the spiritual needs of those we encounter throughout the day. This can happen when we, as good stewards, rely wholly on His provision.

*So do not worry, saying, "What shall we eat?" or "What shall we drink?" or "What shall we wear?"...But seek first His Kingdom and His righteousness, and all these things will be given to you as well.*

—Matthew 6:31,33

A few years back, the intended purpose of my work began to shift from growing my own kingdom to allowing God to use me to grow His Kingdom. Others in our organization have experienced the same. This does not mean we have stopped trying to run an effective and profitable business. On the contrary, it means we have set as our priority the goal to be even better stewards of the resources and relationships that God provides.

For a time, we had a fun-loving group of young equipment salesmen covering the north Georgia region of our territory. They were excellent employees. However, I never really knew where their hearts were. During an economic downturn, all but one of those guys left our company for jobs with greater income potential. I did not know what had become of them until receiving this email:

*Kris,*

*I ran into Paul the other day, and we discussed that you probably don't know what an impact working at Vermeer Southeast has had on our lives. We discussed that sales meeting when you first suggested the idea of SHINE to our sales team. The night before, many of the guys had gone out partying, and as Paul sat there with a hangover, listening to you talk about serving others and honoring God through your work, he made a commitment to be more responsible and intentional about letting his light shine before men.*

*Because the company leadership openly promoted prayer and spiritual growth in the workplace, Paul invited Eric and Greg to pray with him and go to church with him. You have seen the depth in*

*Monte as he's grown into a Christian leader in your company, in his church, and in his household. He has taken that accountability to a new level with his group: to shine.*

*As you know, other than Monte, we have moved on to other jobs, but we still carry the SHINE vision with us. We understand how we can make an eternal difference, and we now openly talk about God and what He is doing in our lives.*

*I don't think you'll ever know until you get to heaven how many people have been impacted by your equipment dealership. You never preached to us, but you laid out what God placed on your heart was a vision to SHINE for Christ. God took it from there, and now others are doing the same in other companies. Who will ever know how many lives will be changed because of SHINE? I just wanted to let you know how our time working with you has changed our lives.*

*Love ya, dude,*

*Scott*

# PURPOSE OF STEWARDSHIP

Personally, I had little to do with changing these men's lives. Jesus Christ clearly did that. By the power of His Spirit, he impacts other lives through us. Over time, we have learned that nothing we experience in life compares to being used by God for His Kingdom purposes. Likewise, there is no greater role we could hope to fulfill than that of a faithful steward chosen by God to co-labor with Him. When God shines through our souls, He is honored, His glory is reflected in us, needs are met through us, and His Kingdom advances. Faithful stewardship allows us to become conduits through which God's bountiful blessings flow.

*Now all glory to God, who is able, through His mighty power at work within us, to accomplish infinitely more than we might ask or think.*

—Ephesians 3:20, NLT

# HONOR GOD

Trust—Depend on Him

Gratitude—Thank Him

Stewardship—Serve Him

*A soul of faithfulness obeys God's purpose.*

# IMPROVE CONTINUALLY

*Enter through the narrow gate. For wide is the gate and broad is the road that leads to destruction, and many enter through it. But small is the gate and narrow the road that leads to life, and only a few find it.*

—MATTHEW 7:13–14

## CHAPTER 9

# Ignite the Flame of Excellence

## A MIND OF EXCELLENCE PURSUES GOD'S VISION

*Supplement your faith with a generous provision of moral excellence,*
*and moral excellence with knowledge, and knowledge*
*with self-control, and self-control with patient endurance,*
*and patient endurance with godliness.*

—2 Peter 1:5–6, NLT

As a teenager, I envisioned myself playing professional golf on the PGA tour. You would laugh at that if you played golf with me today. Yet that dream once drove me to excel as a golfer. By high school, my game had improved enough to receive a collegiate golf scholarship. But from the beginning of my college years, many obstacles lined up to divert my attention. I progressively lost the focus and determination required to excel in competitive golf. As my vision for excellence waned, my progress in the sport halted. Eventually, I gave up on that dream.

Upon graduating from college, I took a job at my dad's company. He needed employees, and I needed a job. So it seemed like a natural fit. My first role was to help wherever needed. My unofficial title was "gopher"—go for this, go for that. My position was at the bottom of the totem pole, which was exactly where I belonged. My mind was not in it at all. I had no passion for the equipment business. It is no surprise that my performance as an employee was far from excellent.

One day, while shamelessly slacking off, I overheard some of my fellow employees talking. No one knew I was listening from the next room. They were discussing how worthless I was. They all agreed that I would never amount to anything and that the only reason I had a job in the first place was because my dad owned the company.

The obstacles were stacking up again.

Fortunately, this time, the obstacles did not stop me. Instead, they sparked a new dream. At that moment, a passion to improve myself was born within me. My new dream was to prove to those employees how much better I could run this business than anyone else, including my dad. This newfound dream proved quite a motivator for me. Nobody would ever again point to nepotism as the reason for my employment.

This kind of motivation was admittedly off base. However, it did kick-start in me an insatiable drive for excellence, which was fueled by continual improvement. I studied, learned, and worked hard… doing whatever it would take to move ahead. Pursuing this dream with great passion eventually led to a high level of personal success. However, what appeared as outwardly fulfilling a dream of excellence ultimately felt empty inside.

Eventually, I learned that true fulfillment is found in seeking God's vision for our lives rather than in chasing our own dreams. His vision for us reaches beyond our dreams and take us to a higher level of excellence. As the focus of our pursuits shifts from chasing our dreams to seeking God's vision, our capacity to grow and improve exponentially increases. When Christ shines in us, we better represent His Kingdom on earth. Nothing could be more excellent than that.

> *But you are a chosen race, a royal priesthood, a holy nation,*
> *a people for his own possession, that you may proclaim the*
> *excellencies of him who called you out of darkness*
> *into his marvelous light.*
>
> —1 Peter 2:9

# AN EXCELLENT WITNESS

When we give our best for His glory, excellence is the result. Let me propose another definition of excellence: *excellence* is using God's gifts to our fullest potential while carrying out the plans He has designed for us.

It is important to note that excellence does not happen automatically. It is not a gift or something into which we are born. Rather, excellence is something we are called to pursue passionately as we live out our days. Excellence does not happen overnight. It is the result of consistently striving to maximize our gifts and talents for God's glory.

Whatever we are called to do, excellence is an integral part of God's plan for us. Yet I know of numerous employers who intentionally shy away from hiring Christians because they have found many to be underperformers at work. A friend of mine owned a large company in the United Kingdom. He recently relayed his disappointment in the fact that many of the professing Christians he employed were some of his poorest employees, often lacking motivation and work ethic. Knowing that he, too, was a Christian, they presumptuously took advantage of their boss's shared faith, viewing their jobs as entitlement, rather than as opportunity.

As ambassadors for Christ, our lives at work are critical to our Christian witness. As believers, we should be keenly aware that our work is under constant scrutiny by those around us. Our work should reflect the excellence of our Lord. Lazy, complaining, underperforming workers do not generate interest in the message of Christ. However, for those who shine with excellence as they serve the Lord, the influence of their work will draw positive attention. We are called to represent God's way in all we do. For that reason alone, Christians should stand out as top employees in any work setting.

*Do everything without complaining and arguing, so that no one can criticize you. Live clean, innocent lives as children of God, shining like bright lights in a world full of crooked and perverse people.*

—Philippians 2:14–15, NLT

# AN EXCELLENT MIND

If the quality of your work is not defined by excellence, it is time to change your thinking. Excellence starts as a thought in our minds. It is estimated that nearly ten thousand thoughts go through the human mind on any given day. All our actions, whether good or bad, begin first as a thought. What we think about is the precursor for what we do. Through prayer, Scripture reading, and our pursuit of God's will, the Holy Spirit fills our minds with excellent thoughts: "*Those who live according to the sinful nature have their minds set on what that nature desires; but those who live in accordance with the Spirit have their minds set on what the Spirit desires*" (Rom. 8:5).

The sinful nature diverts our minds away from God's view of

excellence. Prideful, negative, and selfish thoughts are all produced by the sinful nature. Contrarily, the Spirit supplies just, godly, and excellent thoughts. What do you think about at work? Are you being led by the Spirit? Or does the sinful nature seem to control your mind? Only by the power of the Spirit can we overcome the sinful nature and rise above our negative thoughts.

> *The peace of God, which transcends all understanding, will guard your hearts and your minds in Christ Jesus. Finally, brothers, whatever is true, whatever is noble, whatever is right, whatever is pure, whatever is lovely, whatever is admirable—if anything is excellent or praiseworthy—think about such things.*
>
> —Philippians 4:7–8

Let me lay this out more clearly. How often do you guard your heart and mind by thinking like Christ? How often are your thoughts…

- True?
- Noble?
- Right?
- Pure?
- Lovely?
- Admirable?
- Excellent?

## AN EXCELLENT VISION

Controlling our thoughts is paramount because our thoughts generate our dreams. It is our dreams that inspire us to look ahead. Yet as inspiring as dreams can be, it is important to note that there is a big difference between chasing a dream and seeking God's vision. Our human minds can dream dreams. However, only God can reveal His vision. Because dreams can be so motivating, it is essential that the dreams we pursue line up with God's vision. For instance, there is a big difference between dreaming about achieving great wealth so we can live an extravagant lifestyle versus dreaming that God will bless us financially so we can provide for our families and help fund the advancement of His Kingdom. To be sure a dream is on the right track, ask yourself this simple question: "If I realize this dream, will God be glorified?"

· · · · · · · · · · · · · · · · · · · · · · · · · · · · · · · · · · · · · · · · · · · · · · ·

## *Will God be glorified?*

· · · · · · · · · · · · · · · · · · · · · · · · · · · · · · · · · · · · · · · · · · · · · · ·

The following email I received years ago from Monte, now one of our top leaders, exemplifies the potential excellence of a Kingdom-focused vision:

> *Kris,*
>
> *I woke up this morning at about 3:30 a.m. with this message weighing on my heart. I have to admit, when you first rolled out our new vision statement, "To Shine with Excellence," years ago, I felt it would become just like most of the other vision statements from companies...a catchy phrase with no buy-in from the people.*
>
> *Well, I could not have been more wrong. To watch the growth of our company since God planted that vision within you has been*

*incredible. The neat thing is, when I say "growth," I don't just mean the type of growth that is measured by profit at the end of the year (although that has happened, too). I am talking about the personal and spiritual growth of the employees of this company. I have witnessed it in the lives of many.*

*Most importantly I have come to know Jesus Christ as my personal Lord and Savior. It's one thing to hear about Christ on Sunday, but to see His principles lived out in the workplace is a very powerful testimony and one that had a big impact on my eventual decision to follow Him. In addition, SHINE has brought a renewed passion and fulfillment to my work life. It has allowed me to connect the "what I do" with the "why I do it." Now I realize that God has a purpose for all of us. I know that God has placed me right where I am for a reason.*

*There are numerous other ways SHINE has impacted me and those around me. Bottom line is, I'm grateful God has allowed me to be part of this company, and to pursue this vision.*

- Monte

A Kingdom vision glorifies God. It is His vision that inspires and elevates us to excellence beyond our limited comprehension: *"My thoughts are nothing like your thoughts,' says the Lord. 'And my ways are far beyond anything you could imagine. For just as the heavens are higher than the earth, so my ways are higher than your ways and my thoughts higher than your thoughts'"* (Isa. 55:8–9, NLT).

God is overseeing our constant growth and using our capacity for improvement to prepare us for eternity. A Kingdom vision of excellence continually increases competence, inspires courage, and ignites passion so the excellence of God's Kingdom is clearly reflected in all we do.

## CHAPTER 10

# Shine with Competence

## SOAR WITH STRENGTHS

*Do you see any truly competent workers?*

*They will serve kings rather than working for ordinary people.*

—Proverbs 22:29, NLT

Our company was founded by two young men who grew up on farms in central Iowa. My dad had become the office manager for Vermeer Corporation, and his business partner Mel was a sales representative, who covered the southeast United States. In 1967, they joined forces to start Vermeer Southeast. I do not know if a better business partnership could exist. They both were hard working, committed to running a business by biblical principles, and agreed that caring for people was one of their most important objectives.

My dad was into details, profit, and office/administration. Mel was mechanical, relational, and sales-focused. They knew each other's strengths and respected each other. I am not aware of their ever having an argument regarding the business. They worked in their areas of competence and covered for each other's weaknesses. They were naturally equipped to grow something from the ground up.

As the next generation of leadership—Todd, Jim, and I—took control in 1999, we, too, were very different from each other. My strengths led to a focus on leadership, front-line strategy, and revenue growth. Jim focused on operational process, administration, and back office. Todd's strengths allowed for a focus on sales/profit, marketing, and inventory management. Our diversity of strengths worked well when we stayed in our lanes. Admittedly, we experienced our fair share of friction when our lanes would merge. Thankfully, the three of us found common ground in our faith, our desire to operate by biblical principles, and our care for our employees. This allowed us to rise above the disagreements our differences would create. We were naturally equipped to build teams, implement processes, and expand the business.

As we build the leadership team that will take Vermeer Southeast to a new level in the future, a focus on strengths and core competency has led the way. It is important that our leaders know their strengths and weaknesses and understand those of their teammates as well. Strengths-based leadership is a strategic way to grow a company into the future. This concept is nothing new. It is how Christ has built His Church over all these years.

*There are different kinds of spiritual gifts, but the same Spirit is the source of them all. There are different kinds of service, but we serve the same Lord. God works in different ways, but it is the same God who does the work in all of us. A spiritual gift is given to each of us so we can help each other.*

*—1 Corinthians 12:4–7*

# DEFINE STRENGTHS

God has created each of us with unique strengths and abilities. We shine when we grow these God-given strengths and use them for His glory. Understanding our strengths is critical if we desire to improve continually.

To help stimulate growth, I like to ask people what their three areas of greatest strength are. A frequent response is "I don't know" or "I have never thought about that." Sometimes, people are careful not to tout their strengths because they do not want to appear as braggadocios or arrogant.

Here is something to consider: the reason you have strengths is because God has gifted you in those areas. When we realize that our strengths are gifts from God, we find that acknowledging and using these strengths provide opportunities to please Him. One of the most important things we can do for our own personal growth is to define our God-given strengths. Knowing one's strengths is crucial for any type of improvement.

Take a moment to consider and jot down the three areas of your work in which you are the strongest. (For example, mine are leadership, communication, and coaching.)

1. _____

2. _____

3. _____

Next, ask friends, family, and fellow workers to tell you what they consider to be your top three areas of giftedness. Then compare their lists to yours. These exercises can be fun and can provide you with valuable information. Once your greatest strengths are defined, you should concentrate the majority of your focus on developing and maximizing those areas. Think about ways you can improve your competence in the areas of strength you have listed.

Unwittingly, at a young age, we are conditioned not to focus on our strengths but on our weaknesses. If a child is good at reading but bad at math, teachers place the emphasis on improving the child's math aptitude. Consequently, in this instance, more time is devoted to improving math skill and less to improving reading skills. This may be necessary for developing a well-rounded sphere of knowledge. However, when we get into the work force, many of us reflexively think we need to be well-rounded if we want to be successful. This is just not true. The most successful workers are those who instinctively focus their energies in the areas of their greatest giftedness.

If you are in a supervisory role, one of the most important ways to promote improvement is to help those whom you lead to know and grow their God-given strengths. This is a core competency of leadership. Point out the greatness in friends by simply telling them something you admire about them. Tell them about a God-given strength you have observed in them.

## ACCEPT WEAKNESSES

I often ask prospective employees to tell me about their weaknesses. It is amazing how uncomfortable this makes some people, especially in a job-interview setting. Their responses tell me a lot about them. The fact is, we all have weaknesses. Trying to deny them or cover them up greatly reduces our potential for self-improvement.

Early in my career, while desperately trying to prove myself, I was under the false assumption that I needed to be great at everything to get ahead. I was trying to be everything to everybody. Of course,

I was not successful in doing so. I can still recall the cynical smirks when I finally admitted that I was not very good at many things. What to me seemed like a breakthrough of newly discovered truth was my acknowledging what everyone else already knew: I really stink at certain things!

When we acknowledge our weaknesses to those around us, rarely is it considered new information. Admitting weaknesses does not draw attention to our flaws as much as it displays the inner strength found in self-realization.

List three of your weaknesses at work. (For example, mine are attention to detail, administration, and mechanical aptitude.)

1. _____

2. _____

3. _____

After listing your weaknesses, think about ways you can work around those weaknesses rather than allowing them to hold you back.

The Bible tells us not to hide or be ashamed of our weaknesses but to acknowledge them with confidence in God's power to help us overcome them. *"'My grace is all you need. My power works best in weakness.' So now I am glad to boast about my weaknesses, so that the power of Christ can work through me"* (2 Corin. 12:9, NLT).

God creates each of us with strengths and with weaknesses. It is part of His plan to use His strength—despite our weakness—for His glory. Now that you have defined your strengths and listed your weaknesses, take a moment to pray. Ask the Lord to maximize your strengths and to help you in your areas of weaknesses. Ask Him to use both your strengths and weaknesses for His glory.

# MANAGE WEAKNESSES

In *Soar with Your Strengths*, authors Donald Clifton and Paula Nelson write, "What would happen if we studied what was right with people versus what's wrong with people? Instead of focusing in on what your child or your employees don't do well, the emphasis would be on helping them do more of what they are good at and at managing their weak areas."[1]

So often, we evaluate people based on what they do poorly instead of on what they do well. It is so easy to let weaknesses dominate our improvement efforts. For instance, our company's top leaders are all highly qualified, top-performing employees. Each of them is unique in the strengths and abilities he or she brings to the team. Some are people-focused, and some are task-focused. Some are strong in sales and some in operations. However, none of them are equally strong in all the areas of their job responsibilities. It would be easy to point out their deficiencies and ask them to focus strictly on improving those weaknesses. However, that approach would only limit their growth. It would stifle their creativity and limit their potential for improvement.

Instead, we encourage each of them to work with others on the team to offset their weaknesses. This allows them to spend more time focused on and maximizing their own God-given strengths. Based on their strengths, they all approach their jobs in different ways. Yet each of them accomplishes their objectives because they delegate and work with others to shore up their weaknesses. By focusing on their strengths and managing their weaknesses, our company runs much more effectively than if we expected everyone to do the job exactly the same way.

---

1. Donald O. Clifton and Paula Nelson, *Soar with Your Strengths* (New York: Dell Publishing, 1992), 20–21.

# SOAR WITH STRENGTHS

*Competence* is the combination of our knowledge, skills, and work habits. Improving in these areas leads to high performance. Top performers are never satisfied with the way things currently are. They continually seek improvement in what they do. A vision of excellence does not allow us to ever "arrive" or to know it all. No matter how much we know or achieve, there is always more to learn and areas in which to improve. The author of Proverbs wrote, *"A wise man will hear and increase learning, and a man of understanding will attain wise counsel"* (Prov. 1:5, NKJV).

· · · · · · · · · · · · · · · · · · · · · · · · · · · · · · · · · · ·

*Commitment to personal improvement*

*always precedes corporate*

*improvement.*

· · · · · · · · · · · · · · · · · · · · · · · · · · · · · · · · · · ·

For a company to improve continually, the process begins in the mind of each employee. A commitment to personal improvement always precedes corporate improvement. If you are, or desire to be, in a leadership position, the most important thing you can do for those you aspire to lead is to improve yourself. As you grow in competence—as you set the example for others to seek improvement—you become more valuable to those around you.

Do not sit around and wait for someone to help you improve. Take the initiative. Right now, you can take a positive step by listing three things you can do in the next thirty days to improve your competence at work. In the space provided below, write a commitment you will make to improve in these three areas of competence:

1. Increase knowledge: _____

2. Develop skills: _____

3. Improve work habits: _____

Increasing our knowledge, skills, and work habits leads us to reach our God-given potential. The more we grow in competence, the more we are equipped to reveal His excellence.

> *Never be lazy, but work hard and serve the Lord enthusiastically.*
> —Romans 12:11, NLT

## CHAPTER 11

# Shine with Courage

## TAKE ACTION

*Have I not commanded you? Be strong and of good courage;
do not be afraid, nor be dismayed for the Lord your God
is with you wherever you go.*

—Joshua 1:9, NKJV

Patrick was turned down twice for jobs at Vermeer Southeast. The second time, he told our manager, Monte, "That's okay, but I know I will work for you someday."

Patrick's prophecy came true—a few months later, he began his sales career in north Georgia. "I don't know why," Patrick recalls, "I just knew I was supposed to work here. I didn't know a single thing about sales, but I felt like God was pushing me to step out of my comfort zone and take a chance."

Hard work and a relentless attitude propelled Patrick to strong success in sales. Soon he and his newlywed wife, Anna, moved to Jacksonville, Florida, so Patrick could advance his career. "At first she hated it there," said Patrick. "In fact, I don't think she liked me too much at the time, either. If not for Monte and his support, I don't know what may have come of my career or my marriage. Eventually, we agreed that no matter how bad it seemed, that God had us here for a reason. We knew He had a plan for us. We needed to look beyond our problems and look ahead to solutions by trusting God with our future."

Eventually, life brightened for Patrick and Anna as north Florida began to feel like home. Patrick improved steadily in his work and became sales manager for the region. They had found a church home and were blessed with two beautiful children. Life was grand. But, then it happened again.

Patrick was approached with the opportunity to become our company's youngest regional manager. The promotion would require a move to Birmingham, Alabama. "At first, I was scared," Patrick admitted. "I had only been in sales my entire career. Now I was looking at overseeing not only sales but also service and operations for an entire region. Plus, my family now loved it in north Florida."

After much prayer and consideration Patrick again felt God leading him to pursue growth by moving north and taking on this new challenge. "This company has invested so much in me both at work and at home. I've grown so much both professionally and spiritually. I knew taking this next step would not be easy. But I also knew God was in it and because of that, it would be the right thing to do."

Like Patrick and Anna, God gives us all gifts and talents that He wants us to grow and improve for His glory. When we turn to God, He gives us the courage to pursue change, face fears, look ahead, and take action.

# PURSUE CHANGE

"Don't rock the boat." "Take the path of least resistance." "We have always done it this way." "It's going well now." "Why change?" "It's company policy."

Do any of these statements sound familiar? They are credos of the status quo. Cried out from that dangerous pit called the comfort zone, they are the enemy of improvement—the building blocks of mediocrity.

Improving continually requires courage to do the following:

- Try new things.
- Step out of the comfort zone.
- Embrace change.
- Pursue a vision of excellence.

In the book *Built to Last*, a study of enduring, top companies—companies founded before 1900 and still thriving one hundred years later—authors Jim Collins and Jerry Porras point out the important role change plays in making a great company: "Indeed, if there is any one secret to an enduring great company, it is the ability to manage continuity and change—a discipline that must be consciously practiced, even by the most visionary of companies."[1]

· · · · · · · · · · · · · · · · · · · · · · · · · · · · · · · · · · · · · · · · · · ·

*It is essential to seek positive change and continually step beyond the comfort zone.*

· · · · · · · · · · · · · · · · · · · · · · · · · · · · · · · · · · · · · · · · · · ·

1. Jim Collins and Jerry Porras, *Built to Last* (New York: Harper Collins, 1994), xv.

The courage to change is a critical requirement for a company that desires to grow and improve. Continual progress requires ongoing change. Change is inevitable and cannot be stopped. Proactively negotiating change is key to a successful life at work. In business, it is essential to seek positive change and continually step beyond the comfort zone. Collins and Porras write, "Comfort is not the objective in a visionary company. Indeed, visionary companies install powerful mechanisms to create discomfort—to obliterate complacency—and thereby stimulate change and improvement before the external world demands it."[2]

## FACE FEARS

Seeking God's vision of excellence can be scary. His vision often requires us to step beyond our comfort zone, rise above fear, and triumph over discouragement. It tests our faith and reveals what we believe about Him. The Bible encourages us: "Be on your guard; stand firm in the faith; be men of courage; be strong" (1 Corin. 16:13).

The statement fear not or do not be afraid appears over 300 times in Scripture. The command to fear God appears as many times. The correlation is simple: When we fear the Lord, there is no reason to fear anything else.

*The Lord is my light and my salvation—whom shall I fear?*
*The Lord is the stronghold of my life—of whom shall I be afraid?*
—Psalm 27:1

God is greater than the sum of all our fears. Fear of the Lord inspires the courage to face fears and take action. We gain strength, courage, and confidence each time we face our fears and step out in faith.

---

2. Ibid, 187.

A few years ago, an industry consultant was working with our company to train employees and discuss potential changes in our management structure. I shared with this consultant my desire to use Matthew 5:16 for our company vision. He told me that although he personally agreed with the concept, he, as a consultant, could not advise building a corporate vision statement around a passage of Scripture. He warned that it could offend people and create division. He felt that we would likely lose employees and customers if we did it. He likened it to painting a big target on our company and setting ourselves up for undue scrutiny, criticism, and failure. His advice was to let God continue to guide my personal life, but to keep any public reference to God away from the business. His advice was reasonably sound, from a strictly business perspective. He had done his job as a business consultant: accentuating my primary fears of failure, criticism, and inadequacy. His advice provided me with an easy way out.

God, however, does not desire that we take the easy way out. He wants us to face our fears, trust in Him, and step out boldly to glorify Him. We are not called to a life of comfort but one of courage and confidence in Him. In this case, God's Word was the only business consultant we needed. It is His Word that guides us to truth and ultimate fulfillment. His Word, indeed, should frame all our hopes, dreams, and visions. Without trusting His Word, fear would reign, and we would all miss out. I would hate to think where our company or I would be today had we not looked ahead and relied on Him for the courage to face any fears and seek His vision.

## LOOK AHEAD

There has never been a vision-caster like Jesus Christ. His vision passes the test of time and continues to inspire infinitively. The vision of His Kingdom motivates those who love and trust Him to look ahead and pursue eternal rewards: "For the Son of Man is going to come in His Father's glory with His angels, and then He will reward each person according to what he has done" (Matt. 16:27).

Often, seeking His vision will require us to face challenges, forgo immediate rewards, and, by faith, look ahead. We can take heart when the challenges are lofty and look ahead with courage. For those who seek His vision, the promise of eternal blessing prevails.

Scripture records that before Jesus cast the vision for His followers to shine for His glory, He encouraged believers to look ahead to blessings that will come from pursuing His vision. The Beatitudes, found in the beginning of the fifth chapter of Matthew, offer a brilliant framework on which to structure our thinking in life and at work:

- *"Blessed are the poor in spirit, for theirs is the kingdom of heaven"* (Matt. 5:3). We must become poor in our own spirit to become rich in His Spirit. Make God the boss. Trust Him and look ahead to the blessings of His Kingdom.

- *"Blessed are those who mourn, for they will be comforted"* (Matt. 5:4). People are hurting all around us. Care for them. Mourn for them. Mourning is a part of life on earth. Turn to Him and look ahead to the blessing of comfort.

- *"Blessed are the meek, for they will inherit the earth"* (Matt. 5:5). Humble yourself before God. The humble will receive God's strength. They can look ahead, with confidence, to the blessing of exaltation.

- *"Blessed are those who hunger and thirst for righteousness, for they will be filled"* (Matt. 5:6). Be God-centered and rely on His righteousness to consistently do the right thing. Passionately pursue God's vision and look ahead to a life filled with blessing.

- *"Blessed are the merciful, for they will be shown mercy"* (Matt. 5:7). Care for others. Be forgiving as we have been forgiven. Generously meet the needs of others. Look ahead to the blessing of being cared for ourselves.

- *"Blessed are the pure in heart, for they will see God"* (Matt. 5:8). Become more Christ-like. Others will see Christ in us when we are pure in heart. Look ahead to the blessing of beholding Him face to face.

- *"Blessed are the peacemakers, for they will be called sons of God"* (Matt. 5:9). Be a positive influence. Promote forgiveness over retribution. Relentlessly promote His truth and peace. Through prayer, resolve conflict and confidently face confrontations. Look ahead to the blessings that are yours as a child of God.

- *"Blessed are those who are persecuted because of righteousness, for theirs is the kingdom of heaven"* (Matt. 5:10). Regardless of circumstances, pursue God's vision. Focus beyond challenges and what others may say about your faith. Always seek His righteousness. Look ahead to the blessing of eternal reward.

- *"Blessed are you when people insult you, persecute you and falsely say all kinds of evil against you because of me. Rejoice and be glad, because great is your reward in heaven"* (Matt. 5:11–12a). When obstacles line the path and people try to derail your witness, take courage, rise above, and with great joy, look ahead to the exciting blessings and rewards awaiting those who seek His Kingdom.

# TAKE ACTION

Continuing with Patrick's story from the beginning of this chapter, his early days in his new role proved quite difficult. Along with uprooting his young family, the challenges of managing the Alabama/ Florida panhandle region were stacking up against him. Initially, it looked as if everything could be falling apart. However, Patrick faced each challenge with prayer and confidence. He focused on building relationships with employees and customers.

Patrick courageously made many tough calls. Before long, he built the trust and respect of those around him. One long-term employee shared with me, "When Patrick first showed up here, we wondered who is this kid and what are they thinking? How can this kid possibly be a regional manager? But over time we saw how he treated people and handled challenges. He's proven he is the right person for the job, and we are all very thankful for him."

As Patrick would attest, when challenges come our way the best thing we can do is turn to the Lord, seek His courage, and then take decisive action.

*For I can do everything through Christ, who gives me strength.*
—Philippians 4:13, NLT

Whatever we do in work and in life, God's vision compels us to move forward despite our fears and inadequacies. Regardless of the task at hand, have the courage to give it your all, and always be open to the new path where His vision may lead you. The road can be rocky, and the way often narrows as we stumble along. Seeking His vision often brings us to our knees which is right where God wants us to be. It is there we find the courage to take action.

## CHAPTER 12

# Shine with Passion

## EMPOWER YOUR POTENTIAL

*I focus on this one thing: Forgetting the past and looking forward to what lies ahead, I press on to reach the end of the race and receive the heavenly prize for which God, through Christ Jesus, is calling us.*

—Philippians 3:13–14, NLT

I remember the day I almost burned out. My stress level was maxed, and I was ready to tap out. I had just returned home from a long and draining business trip that had culminated in my dismissing a long-term employee for whom I cared deeply. As I walked through the door, I could sense that my wife, Robin, was equally stressed. It had been a long week with our three young children. The kids were waiting in their rooms for me to "father" them. Robin reminded me that as the head of our household, it was my responsibility to set the level of discipline in our family and that my recent performance in that role had been lacking.

Later that evening, I sat alone and exhausted, with the weight of my responsibilities overwhelming me. I felt like I was failing on all counts. Beyond being a husband, parent, and son—all priorities I believe should come before my work—I was the CEO of a growing business, the president of our dealers association, and president of the financial board of my church. I was serving on two ministries' advisory boards as well. In addition, I was in the process of writing a book. Having so many demanding responsibilities on my plate, I was obviously falling short in my quest for a "balanced life." With my efforts seemingly sinking on all fronts, I cried out to God, "I'm done! I need You! Please provide me with more balance in my life."

It was then that God zapped me with the realization of His omniscient truth. I was chasing after the wrong thing. Balance does not lead to excellence. It only produces mediocrity. Balance does not inspire courage. It only promotes complacency. Balance does not spark the fuel of passion. Rather, while we are chasing after it, balance eventually consumes all our energy. We are not called to a life of balance. We are called to love God with every ounce of energy He provides. Balance is not our target. Radical passion for Christ is the target we should be aiming for.

The many "good things" I was trying to accomplish were getting in the way of my passion for the Lord. When we love Him with all that we are—with heart, soul, mind, and strength—the result is passion: *"'No eye has seen, no ear has heard, no mind has conceived what God has prepared for those who love Him.' But God has revealed it to us by His Spirit..."* (1 Corin. 2:9–10).

That evening, God clearly revealed that I should be growing and improving my passion for Him, above all other priorities. When my relationship with Him is my top priority, His passion for excellence overflows in me and, in turn, helps energize and prioritize all areas of responsibility in my life. The truth is, we cannot possibly balance our lives on our own. However, God helps us balance our lives if we make Him our top priority and rely on Him as our true passion.

# PASSION RELEASES POWER

Above many other qualities, passion is one of the most powerful. God-given passion inspires significant lives that leave a legacy. If you really want to improve in a certain area, raise your level of passion in that area. To reach for your full potential, focus on your areas of competence, have the courage to take action despite obstacles, and strive to improve continually by passionately pursuing a vision of excellence.

About passion, best-selling leadership author John Maxwell wrote, "Experts spend a lot of time trying to figure out what makes people successful. They often look at people's credentials, intelligence, education, and other factors. But more than anything else, passion makes the difference."[1]

How passionate are you about life and work? Are you filled with passion, or is your tank drained? The good news is that the source of passion stands ready to fill you up at any time.

*Ask and it will be given to you; seek and you will find; knock and the door will be opened to you. For everyone who asks receives; he who seeks finds; and to him who knocks, the door will be opened.*
—Luke 11:9–10

Passion is powered by these key components:

- Desire (ask)
- Discipline (seek)
- Determination (knock)

---

1. John Maxwell, *The 21 Indispensable Qualities of a Leader* (Nashville, TN: Thomas Nelson, 1999).

# DESIRE AND DISCIPLINE FUEL PASSION

Desire drives passion. How much we want something generally determines how hard we are willing to work for it. The greater the desire, the hotter the fire of passion will burn within us. Desire stimulates the willpower to pursue a vision of excellence. Passionate people continually display an unyielding desire for growth and progress. Growth-oriented, passionate individuals continually seek to be better tomorrow than they are today, to improve more next week than they did this week, and to be stronger next year than they are now. Scripture instructs that we should seek God as the driving force behind our desires: *"Grow in the grace and knowledge of our Lord and Savior Jesus Christ..."* (2 Peter 3:18).

Regardless of our level of giftedness, we will never reach our full potential without the continual application of self-discipline. Passion is not found in busyness and frantic activity but in the focused discipline of doing a few things with passion and focused excellence. *"For God has not given us a spirit of fear and timidity, but of power, love, and self-discipline"* (2 Tim. 1:7, NLT).

One of the key elements of the top-performing companies profiled in Jim Collins's book *Good to Great* is that each great company had created a unique culture of discipline that effectively drove the organization toward continual improvement and enduring success. Collins wrote, "A culture of discipline is not just about action. It is about getting disciplined people who engage in disciplined thought and who then take disciplined action."[2]

---

2. Collins, *Good to Great,* 142.

# DETERMINATION FULFILLS PASSION

Determination is firmness of purpose, will, and intention. It is needed to finish a race, to complete a task, and to improve continually. A vision of excellence focused on growth will always require effort and determination. *"Don't you realize that in a race everyone runs, but only one person gets the prize? So run to win"* (1 Corin. 9:24, NLT). Determination allows us to overcome obstacles that mark our paths. In fact, determination transforms obstacles from the excuses that hold us back into the motivations that inspire us to forge ahead.

Be determined to keep asking, seeking, knocking, and glorifying God in all you do. Take a moment to feel the determined passion that the apostle Paul expresses in Philippians 3:13–14 (NLT): *"I focus on this one thing: Forgetting the past and looking forward to what lies ahead, I press on to reach the end of the race and receive the heavenly prize for which God, through Christ Jesus, is calling us."*

Paul wrote this message from jail while drawing close to death. Despite his surroundings and all the accomplishments of his life's work, he chose not to look back but to look ahead to eternal glory. He still hungered for growth and improvement. Paul chose to passionately pursue his full potential in Christ Jesus.

- Paul displayed competence and desire as he focused on what he did best: *"I focus on this one thing"* (Phil. 3:13b, NLT).

- Paul modeled the courage and discipline to look ahead, regardless of circumstances: *"Forgetting the past and looking forward to what lies ahead"* (Phil. 3:13c, NLT).

- Paul showed that his passion and determination were unwavering: *"I press on to reach the end of the race and receive the heavenly prize"* (Phil. 3:14a, NLT).

- Paul passionately pressed on in the pursuit of God's vision of excellence: *"For which God, through Christ Jesus, is calling us"* (Phil. 3:14b, NLT).

The passion that God provides is contagious. Like Paul, when we are filled with God's passion, it not only fills us but overflows and impacts others. Passion lifts us beyond our fears and lack of abilities. It inspires us to do things in Him that we could not imagine doing on our own.

# PASSION EMPOWERS POTENTIAL

When we consider our own potential, we naturally tend to think in finite terms. We all have potential to grow and improve. With vision, we can maximize our gifts and talents to reach new levels. However, God sees us with much greater potential than we do. We look at things in our current state. God sees us in the light of eternity. Our potential in Christ reaches beyond the here and now and reaches into the ever-after.

Stephen Covey, the author of *7 Habits of Highly Effective People*, said that if you want to define a compelling vision, begin with the end in mind. Picture in your mind what it will look like to succeed, and strive to reach that vision. Beginning with the end in mind is great advice. However, as Christ followers, I would suggest we go a bit further. Because of the salvation found in Christ, the end of earthly life is not the end for us. It is the beginning of eternity. To pursue a Kingdom vision, look beyond the end, and begin with eternity in mind. God-given passion stretches our potential beyond our own vision and empowers us to seek His higher calling for all eternity.

. . . . . . . . . . . . . . . . . . . . . . . . . . . . . . . . . . . . . . . . .

*When we focus on God's vision of excellence, we not only improve continually but also invest eternally.*

. . . . . . . . . . . . . . . . . . . . . . . . . . . . . . . . . . . . . . . . .

I recall an early vision for our company that was both compelling and impactful. At a time when we were generating around $30 million per year in total sales, I shared a vision of our becoming a $100 million-per-year company. It seemed like a stretch, but that is exactly what vision casting should do. Eventually, we met this benchmark, but it was not nearly as rewarding as I had expected. Looking back, this was a motivating vision that helped our team strive for sales excellence. It was good for a time. Yet it made no lasting impact. The vision was finite.

Setting stretch goals and striving to achieve benchmarks are coveted results of vision. However, these pale in comparison to seeking a Kingdom vision. I am quite sure that when I stand before the Lord one day, He will not care about how much equipment our company sold. However, I do believe that the times we allowed Christ to SHINE in us to impact others will be remembered and rewarded.

Now, that is a vision worth getting passionate about.

When His vision is achieved, it not only makes a difference today but also impacts eternity. When we focus on God's vision of excellence, we not only improve continually; we also invest in eternity. He provides the passion required to pursue His vision. When we serve God with all we have and make loving Him our top priority, He lifts our potential to the infinite, balances our lives as He sees fit, and empowers us by His Spirit to impact eternity.

*Then the godly will shine like the sun in their Father's Kingdom. Anyone with ears to hear should listen and understand.*

—Matthew 13:43, NLT

# IMPROVE CONTINUALLY

Competence—Soar with Strengths

Courage—Take Action

Passion—Empower Your Potential

*A mind of excellence seeks God's vision.*

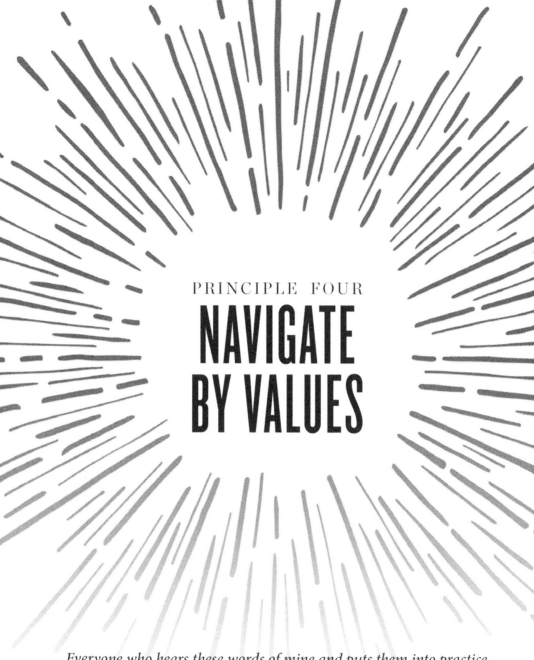

PRINCIPLE FOUR

# NAVIGATE BY VALUES

*Everyone who hears these words of mine and puts them into practice is like a wise man who built his house on the rock. The rain came down, and the streams rose, and the winds blew and beat against that house; yet it did not fall, because it had its foundation on the rock.*

—MATTHEW 7:24–25

## CHAPTER 13

# Ignite the Flame of Integrity

## THE STRENGTH OF INTEGRITY RISES ON GODLY VALUES

*May integrity and honesty protect me, for I put my hope in You.*

—Psalm 25:21, NLT

Mary Vermeer Andringa has been a friend, business associate, and mentor of mine for many years. We have both been afforded the opportunity to follow in our fathers' footsteps. Mary's dad, Gary Vermeer, founded the Vermeer Corporation in 1948, and my dad founded Vermeer Southeast in 1967. Mary also has served as the CEO for Vermeer Corporation during most of my time as CEO at Vermeer Southeast. I have learned much about business and life from her. Most importantly, Mary has exemplified the integrity of running a highly successful business while maintaining a healthy and vibrant family life. I asked her to kick off this chapter by expanding a bit on how powerful navigating by values has been for Vermeer as a whole:

> *As a long-term family member involved in the Vermeer Corporate business, I have seen the importance of understanding your values and communicating those values to your team, to your distribution, and to your customers. As my two brothers and I joined the*

*company in the late '70s and early '80s, it was clear that many of our goals aligned with the corporate values our father had instilled in our organization from the very beginning.*

*As a former schoolteacher, I realized that if we took some of these values and connected them to People, Product, Profit and tied them together with biblical Principles, we would have an easy way to remember our values and talk about them. Those 4 P's have continued to be the foundation of our values and our culture. Knowing the key values of a company can really bring confidence to team members as they do their work and make decisions based on the values of the company. Sharing our values can also build confidence for our independent dealers, suppliers, and our retail customers.*

*It has been especially gratifying to see our dealer organizations understand and promote these values. Vermeer Southeast is exemplary in reflecting values. They have established many best practices around recruiting talent that aligns with their values and setting up great onboarding and development programs, which promote growth and values alignment for every single team member. They also align their values around how they take care of their customers.*

*Recently, I spoke at an association conference about the importance of knowing and sharing your values so that they become the basis of your company culture. In the next couple days, I had several retail customers and vendors tell me that they see a real consistency in Vermeer Corporation and Vermeer dealership team members who display the same culture based on values. I believe this kind of consistency of values speaks well for the greater Vermeer enterprise. Conviction to these values promotes integrity so that all of our constituents across the globe will know what they can expect from Vermeer.*

# THE STRENGTH OF INTEGRITY

If operating with integrity were easy and always produced instant positive results, I am sure more people and businesses would practice it. However, practicing integrity does not come easily and often takes time to produce results. Integrity is revealed over time by continually doing the right things with consistency. True integrity is not about achieving worldly success or praise among people. It is about obeying the commands of God, recognizing His goodness, and walking in step with Him.

When we focus our energy on serving others, honoring God, and improving continually, a great amount of momentum is generated. Momentum enhances performance and increases opportunities. It can make a whole company feel unstoppable. If left unguided, however, momentum can quickly take a person or a company down the wrong path. Navigating by values helps channel momentum in the right direction. Values provide a guardrail, keeping momentum on the right track—the track of integrity.

Navigating by values accomplishes the following:

- Aligns what we do with who we are and unites our performance with our character.

- Merges what we say with what we do and connects our beliefs to our behaviors.

- Helps lead to integrity instead of being duplicitous.

Having integrity—being who we say we are—is about genuineness and authenticity. A painting, for example, is said to have integrity if it proves to have been authentically created by its named artist. A rope has integrity if it can fulfill its purpose of holding a certain amount of weight. People are said to have integrity when they practice what they preach.

Still, integrity is even more than that.

Integrity is based on truth, honor, and reliability. It is wholeness, completeness, and steadfast adherence to the highest of all standards: the character of Christ. A person of integrity can be counted on at all times.

> *Those who are honest and fair, who refuse to profit by fraud, who stay far away from bribes, who refuse to listen to those who plot murder, who shut their eyes to all enticement to do wrong. These are the ones who will dwell on high...*
>
> —Isaiah 33:15–16, NLT

# THE VALUE OF INTEGRITY

Fearing that they can never live up to the high expectation that integrity demands, some individuals are intimidated by the idea of integrity. Yet integrity is not perfection. In reality, there was only one person, Jesus Christ, who lived a fully righteous and perfect life. Because of Jesus, people of integrity do not have to be perfect. They can simply believe in Jesus and follow Him. A person of integrity understands the impossibility of living a perfect life. Our imperfections are, after all, why Jesus died for us. He paid the price for our sins and our deficiencies. Because of Him, we do not have to put on a front of righteousness to win the approval of others. Rather, when we mess up, we can admit our mistakes, seek forgiveness, and move ahead in the confidence that His grace provides.

One of the clearest signs of integrity is when someone readily admits that they did something wrong. Instead of trying to hide it or cover up a mistake, a person of integrity owns up. If this mistake requires repentance, a person of integrity repents. If it requires an apology, a person of integrity apologizes. A person of integrity is strong enough to overcome mistakes by confessing them before God and others. God promises to be there for those who walk with integrity: *"He grants a treasure of common sense to the honest. He is a shield to those who walk with integrity"* (Prov. 2:7, NLT).

We all make mistakes. Yet, regardless of our past, it is never too late to seek forgiveness and, through the strength of a repentant heart, to return to the path of integrity. When we are sincere in our repentance, God promises to forgive us and make us whole again.

Research indicates that the top character quality employees desire in a boss is integrity. In a study sponsored by the American Management Association, fifteen hundred employees were asked what values, traits, or characteristics they admired in their superiors. The most frequent response was integrity.[1] Coincidently, the top characteristic that bosses are looking for in employees is also integrity. And when choosing a company to do business with, people look for integrity.

Based on the important role that integrity plays in the workplace, one would assume that corporate America would be beyond reproach in matters of ethics, morality, and doing the right thing. We all know how far that is from the current reality.

---

1. Greg Farrell and Jayne O'Donnell, "Money Section," *USA Today,* (16 November 2005).

# THE WHOLENESS OF INTEGRITY

Unfortunately, a lack of professional integrity has become far too common in today's marketplace. Many people are willing to "fudge" the truth, to "borrow" from the company, to "make small allowances" for themselves—without feeling any guilt. This comes from an attitude of "they owe it to me" rather than one of "I owe it to them." It could be so different if employees were to adapt the famous John F. Kennedy quote and let it reflect their thinking and actions at work: "Ask not what your [company] can do for you; ask what you can do for your [company]."

I recall a gentleman from my church whom I respected for his seemingly bold faith and compassionate heart. Although I did not know him well, he appeared to be one of those people whom one could admire as a pillar of integrity. I was surprised when more than one of his ex-employees described this man's lack of integrity at work. Over time, I heard more and more about his penchant for cutting corners, cheating customers, and treating his employees poorly. Clearly, this man had been putting on a front of integrity at church while unquestionably compromising his integrity in business. Like so many others, he apparently believed that it was okay to switch integrity on and off based on the situation.

It is not uncommon to find people who claim to have integrity in their personal lives yet compromise their integrity at work to get ahead. This is clear: if you claim to have integrity at home but not at work, you do not have integrity. There is no such thing as having a little bit of integrity. Integrity cannot be divided. It is whole and complete, or it does not exist. You either have integrity or you do not. God does not differentiate the activities of your life. He looks at the whole. He does not apply different standards to business than He does to the rest of your life. The walk of integrity is all-inclusive.

*The integrity of the upright guides them, but the unfaithful are destroyed by their duplicity.*

—Proverbs 11:3

# THE MODEL OF INTEGRITY

God sent the ideal example of integrity in His Son, Jesus Christ. His life on earth provided the perfect model for true integrity:

- What we do (our behavior) is very important.

- Who we are (our character) is even more important.

- Who we are becoming (like Christ) is most important.

Developing Christ-like character builds integrity while making us whole and complete.

I heard a story of an old farmer who took up the hobby of wood carving to pass time during his retirement. Eventually, he grew quite accomplished, and his creations began drawing crowds at the county market. One of his favorite works was a life-sized eagle that he had chiseled from a large log. People marveled over the detail and the skill required in carving such a masterpiece. When asked how he created such a beautiful eagle from a chunk of wood, he responded, "It was easy. I just cut away everything that doesn't look like an eagle."

. . . . . . . . . . . . . . . . . . . . . . . . . . . . . . . . . . . . . . . . .

*The strength of integrity rises*

*on godly values.*

. . . . . . . . . . . . . . . . . . . . . . . . . . . . . . . . . . . . . . . . .

This story provides a fitting analogy of how God develops our character. He already knows what we should look like. When we yield to Christ and seek to personify His values, God purposefully and skillfully cuts away everything in our character that does not look like Jesus Christ. It is through this process that we are formed to become like His Son. We are God's masterpieces. When God works in us, He shapes our character to honor and glorify Him. We can be confident that God acts with integrity because He is faithful in keeping His promise to finish the masterpiece that our lives can be.

> *And I am certain that God, who began the good work*
> *within you, will continue His work until it is finally finished*
> *on the day when Christ Jesus returns.*
>
> —Philippians 1:6, NLT

# IGNITE THE FLAME OF INTEGRITY

As we become more like Christ, our behavior reveals the true values of our God. As we trust God and allow Him to work in us, values of integrity become evident. Navigating by values requires the following:

- Clarity to know what we believe
- Conviction to live out those beliefs
- Confidence to make the right choices

Our journey of faith is a continual process of developing Christ-like values as we become more and more like Him and as His integrity shines through us.

## CHAPTER 14

# Shine with Clarity

KNOW YOUR VALUES

*Now we see things imperfectly as in a cloudy mirror, but then
we will see everything with perfect clarity. All that I know now
is partial and incomplete, but then I will know everything completely,
just as God now knows me completely.*

—1 Corinthians 13:12, NLT

In the early days of Vermeer Southeast, my dad and his partner, Mel, set the example for our company. Their faith, entrepreneurial spirit, and strong work ethic were keys in birthing a successful equipment dealership. Their directing management style formed the parameters for how our company should operate. As the company grew, their entrepreneurial style became difficult to replicate. Employees hired in outlying stores had limited contact with the owners and, therefore, limited guidance on how to perform. Over time, the company basically evolved into two separate organizations: the original locations and the newer stores. The flagship stores, where the owners presided, had clear direction and consistent leadership, while the outlying locations functioned independently, often with uncertainly and inconsistency.

As I began taking a more active role in managing the company, one of my first key responsibilities was to establish written corporate values that would clearly define how we would operate. We did not create new values. Rather, we identified, clarified, and verbalized the values that already existed in our company. We built on the foundation that was already in place.

Clarifying our values helped establish the framework that would allow our company to grow and improve, while maintaining the integrity of its company founders. By articulating our values, we defined the financial, operational, and ethical expectations to our entire organization. This clarity empowered employees to carry out their individual duties while operating within the boundaries of our values and ideals. In essence, the values became the true directors of the organization that provided the clarity to navigate through the daily challenges of work.

# SEEK CLARITY

"I don't know."

Right now, try saying it aloud: "I don't know." Go ahead and say it again: *"I don't know!"* How does that statement make you feel? Is it hard for you to say?

I have found that too many people do not like to say those words. I have observed countless employees and managers who try to fake it—sometimes even making something up instead of admitting they do not know. I believe that most people willingly accept and respect people who admit that they do not know something but are committed to finding it out. Nothing frustrates me personally more than a know-it-all pretender.

Admitting what we do not know is the first step toward finding clarity and a key to developing integrity. "I don't know" is becoming one of my most frequently used statements. Where I once thought knowing everything established an aura of importance, I have come to learn that "I don't know, but let's find out" is much more effective.

No one can know everything or gather all the potential, available information. We live in a fast-paced world full of uncertainty. As we navigate through the challenges of life, we continually will face situations we have never seen before. However, despite the uncertainty, we will be called on to make decisions and move ahead. Consequently, uncertainty can cripple us if we allow it to overly delay critical decisions.

Sometimes it is best to step out in faith and make decisions despite being unsure of the outcome. Taking clear action in the face of uncertainty is a key element of establishing leadership. Uncertainty can either be a restraint that holds us back, or it can be a springboard that launches us forward. Pastor and leadership expert Andy Stanley wrote, "Your capacity as a leader will be determined by how well you learn to deal with uncertainty. Regardless of the type of organization you work in, your future leadership responsibilities will be capped by your ability or inability to manage uncertainty."[1]

In the midst of uncertainty, clarity of values can become a catalyst for clear decisions. Knowing what we believe and clarifying what we value promotes confidence to navigate through the uncertainties of life and work.

---

1. Andy Stanley, *The Next Generation Leader* (Sisters, OR: Multnomah Publishers, 2003), 69.

# CHART YOUR COURSE

Knowing and clarifying our values is essential for living a life of integrity. Values are the core beliefs that we hold dearest and are unwilling to compromise. Clearly defined values are critical for keeping us on track as we pursue our vision. Consider it this way: If you were going somewhere you had never been before, would you just start driving and hope to eventually arrive at your destination? Of course not. Once your destination was determined, you would investigate how to get there. You would map your route and monitor your progress.

Living without clarified values is like driving aimlessly without direction. Navigating by values charts the course that confidently leads you, despite uncertainties.

. . . . . . . . . . . . . . . . . . . . . . . . . . . . . . . . . . . . . . . . . .

*Goals clarify things we would like to accomplish. Values help clarify who we are.*

. . . . . . . . . . . . . . . . . . . . . . . . . . . . . . . . . . . . . . . . . .

I often ask people if they have clearly defined goals they would like to achieve. I have found that most people have clarified specific goals they would like to accomplish. However, when I ask people if they have clearly defined a set of core values to guide them through life, it is a different story. *Goals* clarify things we would like to accomplish. *Values* help clarify who we are. Most of us are more likely to clarify things we would like to do rather than to clarify values, which reveal who we are. Clarity is found by charting a course based on clearly defined values.

# ALIGN YOUR PRIORITIES

*Priorities* reveal what is most important to us. Navigating by values starts by clarifying priorities and then aligning core values with those life priorities. Looking back over my life, I am amazed at how often my core values shifted before I aligned them with my priorities. Because I had never clearly defined my own priorities, I bounced around with no course, no clarity, and no chartable direction. Often, what I valued was whatever seemed best for me at that time. Eventually, God clarified my need to set clear personal values to mark the priorities in my life. As I prayed for God to reveal what my personal core values should be, these life priorities ultimately became clear: faith, family, integrity, and responsibility.

Establishing and living by clear values help me to stay on course and make solid choices. Ultimately, these values guide my decisions. Scripture says, *"The man of integrity walks securely, but he who takes crooked paths will be found out"* (Prov. 10:9).

Let me challenge you to clearly define your own personal core values, if you have never done so. It might take some thought and time to articulate your life priorities. If you are not ready to do so, mark this page, give it some thought, and come back to it soon. Think about what personal values best define the priorities of your life. Write them down and regularly refer to them.

**My Personal Values:**

_____

_____

_____

_____

# SET YOUR SIGHTS

Just as we need personal values to chart the course for our journey, we also need operational values to set the sights for our performance. Operational values should align with personal values to guide us in the proper direction. When operational values line up with personal values, strength of integrity is produced. The Bible instructs us, *"In everything set them an example by doing what is good. In your teaching show integrity, seriousness and soundness of speech that cannot be condemned, so that those who oppose you may be ashamed because they have nothing bad to say about us"* (Titus 2:7–8).

The SHINE vision provides principles that lead to a desired outcome: a work life that glorifies God. Within the vision are operational values to navigate by that keep us on target. These five values provide clarity, focus, and alignment along the path:

| Principle | Operational Value |
|---|---|
| 1. Serve Others | Servanthood |
| 2. Honor God | Faithfulness |
| 3. Improve Continually | Excellence |
| 4. Navigate by Values | Integrity |
| 5. Excel in Relationships | Relationships |

Clarity of values leads to a life of integrity. Take a moment to define your own operational values. What values would you like to guide your performance in life and at work? Either jot them down now, or do so later.

**My Operational Values:**

_____

_____

_____

_____

# KNOW YOUR VALUES

Clarity is essential as we approach the challenges of our work. Personal values lined up with operational values can keep us pointed in the right direction. The following questions can help define clarity in our work:

- What does our company stand for?
- How does our company define success?
- How do I fit in?
- What is expected of me?
- How am I doing?
- How do I get ahead?
- How can I make a difference?

If you are an employer, help your company find clarity by providing answers to these questions for each of your employees. Make it a part of their job descriptions, and evaluate their performance in these areas with regular communication and encouragement.

If you are an employee, ask your boss to clarify expectations for you. It is important for both leaders and employees to clearly understand what is expected and how well those expectations are being met. Seeking clarity and shared values promote teamwork and united direction.

Confession: as a Miami Dolphins fan, I had to look way back to find a winning example regarding my favorite team. All-time NFL victory leader Don Shula—who is especially well known for coaching the Dolphins to a perfect 17–0 season in 1972—wrote, "As a coach, I always carried with me a set of core beliefs, values, and convictions that supported my vision of perfection. These beliefs drove my entire philosophy of coaching. They set the context and boundaries from which players and coaches could operate."[2]

The most successful teams, companies, and individuals are those who plainly understand their core values and clearly communicate them throughout their organizations. Clearly defined values reflect these important factors:

- Who we are

- What we believe

- How we will operate

Building our lives on godly values is much like securely following a map that leads to our desired destination. Godly values allow us to move confidently when the winds, rains, and storms of uncertainty beat upon us. The clarity of godly values sets the course for a life of integrity and directs us through all the competing elements of life. More important than defining who we are, though, the clarity of God's values defines *Whose* we are.

---

2. Don Shula, *The Little Book of Coaching* (New York, NY: Harper Collins, 2001), 11.

*I will bring that group through the fire and make them pure. I will refine them like silver and purify them like gold. They will call on My name, and I will answer them. I will say, "These are My people," and they will say, "The Lord is our God."*

—Zechariah 13:9, NLT

## CHAPTER 15

# Shine with Conviction

## LIVE YOUR VALUES

*For we know, brothers loved by God, that He has chosen you, because our gospel came to you not simply with words, but also with power, with the Holy Spirit and with deep conviction...*

—1 Thessalonians 1:4–5

Faith. Family. Integrity. Responsibility. These are the four personal core values I listed in the previous chapter. Those may sound good at face value; however, they do not mean anything unless I live them out. If we desire to navigate by values, it requires more than just writing them down. Our *actions* prove if we prioritize our values. My good friend Buck Jacobs says, "Priorities are what we do. Everything else is just talk."

Buck is the founder of the C12 Group, the nation's largest network of Christian CEOs, business owners, and executives. C12 Group's mission is to equip Christian CEOs and owners to build greater businesses for a greater purpose. Their vision is to change the world by advancing the Gospel in the marketplace. I joined C12 years ago. The encouragement and accountability I find in my peer advisory group have been invaluable. More than anything, it has helped me stay true to my values and strive to live them out daily.

Buck once challenged me with the simple question, "When do you spend time alone with God?"

"Whenever I can—all throughout the day," I responded with what I thought was a good answer.

"That's great," Buck said, "but have you ever made spending time with God your first priority each day?"

For more than thirty years, Buck has practiced what he calls the most important hour of the day. Each morning, Buck makes it his first priority to spend time alone with God in prayer, reading His Word, and journaling, or as Buck says, "Writing a love letter to God."

Truthfully, up to that point, I had always listed faith in God as my top core value, but I had not made it my first priority. But now, the intentionality of spending the first moments of each day alone with God has proven so life-critical that I recommend it to anyone who desires to live a life of faith.

Saying we have faith does not show conviction. Prioritizing and practicing our faith does. The bottom line is, values are not meant to be words we jot down somewhere or statements that frame the walls of our offices. Values are meant to be seen clearly as we live out our days. Values should be the guardrails that keep us channeled in the right direction. Listing values charts our course. Living values marks a life of impact.

## ACTIONS OVER WORDS

It is not that difficult to say that we have values. Sometimes it even feels good to talk about them. In the previous chapter, we focused on the importance of clarifying values. But all the work of clarifying is useless if all we do is talk about values without acting on them. What we value is seen in our actions, not in our words.

> *What good is it, dear brothers and sisters, if you say you have faith but don't show it by your actions? Can that kind of faith save anyone.*
>
> —James 2:14, NLT

Navigating by values requires deep belief in and conviction to those chosen ideals. Without conviction, our values carry no influence whatsoever. Conviction—more than anything—enables us to live out our values.

One year, as our company compared health-care benefits, one of my business partners, Jim, who oversees insurance, met with potential providers. As the representative of a major health insurance carrier began his sales pitch, Jim noticed the company values printed on the back of this salesperson's business card. At one point, Jim asked the salesperson to expand on the company values. He responded, "That's just something they put on the back of our business cards. I'm not even sure what it says." Talk about a lack of conviction! It was no big surprise when—a few years later—this company experienced rough financial times due to poor service, which drove clients away.

# PERFORMANCE OVER PROMISE

It is important to note that if we are navigating by values, we have to be going somewhere. We do not navigate by sitting still. We navigate while moving ahead. Even if you're on the right track, you could get run over if you just sit there. We do not navigate by proclaiming values. We navigate by *performing* values.

In the business world, the words *morals* and *ethics* are sometimes mentioned. *Morals* are internally focused, and *ethics* are externally focused. Values need to be both. Navigating by values ties what we believe to how we perform our work. These are the written core values of a well-known company:

- Communication

- Respect

- Integrity

- Excellence

You would expect a company with these stated values to be a pretty good place to work. These values could certainly lead a company to enduring success if the organization lived them out. Take a guess which infamous company had clarified these written core values. These are the core values of the Enron Corporation prior to its collapse and bankruptcy.[1]

. . . . . . . . . . . . . . . . . . . . . . . . . . . . . . . . . . . . . .

*We do not navigate by proclaiming values. We navigate by performing values.*

. . . . . . . . . . . . . . . . . . . . . . . . . . . . . . . . . . . . . .

It is painfully obvious that something went wrong along the way. Enron might have clarified these values, but its leaders certainly were

1. Carolyn B. Thompson and James W. Ware, *The Leadership Genius of George W. Bush*, (Hoboken, NJ: John Wiley and Sons, 2003), 18.

not using them for navigation. The tragedy is that the collapse of Enron might have been avoided had the leadership at Enron simply followed its stated values. Many of the actions taken by some Enron employees, which led to its collapse, were completely contrary to the stated values of the company. This lack of conviction eventually led Enron to bankruptcy and cost investors nearly $60 billion in losses.

Is it any surprise that a lack of personal convictions can do the same for us? If we abandon our convictions, we, too, can find ourselves internally bankrupt and adrift in a sea of ethical and moral failure.

# CONVICTION OVER COMPROMISE

One of my favorite stories of conviction is found in Daniel 3. It is the story of three young Hebrew slaves who, due to their excellence and values, rose to prominent roles in the largest enterprise of the time. If they would just go with the flow and do as they were told, they would be set for life. As their boss, the Babylonian king, expanded his empire, he became increasingly prideful. He required all people in his kingdom to worship an idol in reverence to him. Refusal to do so led to a death sentence in a fiery furnace. The three slaves faced a crisis of belief. Outwardly, they had nothing to gain and everything to lose by defying the king's edict. However, these three were strong men of values. They knew that following their boss's order would compromise their own personal values. Refusing to worship the golden idol, the three chose conviction over compromise.

The infuriated king turned up the heat higher than ever before and cast the three slaves into a furnace. Things looked bleak. But then God showed up. He rescued them from the furnace, and the three God-followers emerged from the fire unscathed.

> *Then Nebuchadnezzar said, "Praise be to the God of Shadrach,*
> *Meshach and Abednego, who has sent His angel and rescued His*
> *servants! They trusted in Him and defied the king's command*
> *and were willing to give up their lives rather than serve or worship*
> *any god except their own God." … Then the king promoted*
> *Shadrach, Meshach and Abednego in the province of Babylon.*
>
> —Daniel 3:28, 30

In today's business environment, we might not face fiery furnaces, but we will encounter situations that require conviction about our values. When the fire is hottest, that is when our values are needed the most.

The years 2008–10 was the most challenging time frame I have faced, both personally and professionally. During that period, our company lost more than half our yearly revenues and had to make many difficult organizational changes just to survive. I sent the following email to our team in January 2009:

> *Each new year, I pray for the Lord to reveal a meaningful word*
> *that can help keep me on track for the upcoming 12 months. This*
> *year it is an odd word: cultivate. Let me share my thoughts, as I*
> *believe this word can directly apply to Vermeer Southeast in the*
> *upcoming year. Basically, I see three key elements that relate to the*
> *word cultivate:*
>
> - *Health*
> - *Growth*
> - *Harvest*
>
> ***Health**—In the current economic climate, a focus on health is vital*
> *for our organization. We need to be doing the right things in the*
> *right ways, both operationally and financially. We must maintain*

*health in order to survive today and thrive tomorrow.*

*__Growth__—We need to keep doing the things today that will prepare us for success later. We may need to change a few things now to insure our future. Yet the foundation of our company values will not change. It is on this firm foundation that we remain strong and will grow again. We are working on fertile ground.*

*__Harvest__—Despite what is happening around us today, we need to look ahead with vision and be confident in the harvest that lies ahead. The "N" in SHINE represents "Navigate by Values." Conviction to our values will cultivate health, prepare us for growth, and lead to an eventual harvest.*

*This concept has become very real for me in the last few weeks. As you probably know, my nine-year-old daughter is awaiting a heart transplant. She has been sick to the point of near death. Through this difficult time, God has worked many miracles. We trust He will bring her to a point of health so she can be strengthened for growth, and at the proper time receive a new heart and reap the harvest of a long and meaningful life. Hope is in our hearts. The harvest is in the Lord's hands.*

*Thanks for allowing me to share my word with all of you. I truly believe our greatest days as a company are ahead of us. So, together I propose we stay the course and prepare for rain. We cannot control the economy, but we can choose to cultivate now and trust the future harvest to God.*

Navigating by values is about choosing to live by values, even when it seems difficult. Conviction to values—especially when life gets tough—makes a lasting impact. Scripture tells us, *"Fire tests the purity of silver and gold, but the Lord tests the heart"* (Prov. 17:3, NLT).

## CHAPTER 16

# Shine with Confidence

## TRUST YOUR VALUES

*Blessed is the man who trusts in the Lord, whose confidence*
*is in Him. He will be like a tree planted by the water that sends out its*
*roots by the stream. It does not fear when heat comes; its leaves*
*are always green. It has no worries in a year of drought and*
*never fails to bear fruit.*

—Jeremiah 17:7–8

I was distraught, sitting at the kitchen table with my head buried in my hands. The world was seemingly crashing down around me. The joy of my daughter's miraculous healing was being displaced by the fear of losing our business. For many months, our company had been struggling. I had been doing my best to handle work issues while my heart was focused on tending to Gracyn. When she returned home in May 2009, I settled back into my full-time work.

Our revenue numbers were crashing, and our reserves were drying up. It was time to make some difficult, life-impacting decisions just to stay afloat. We needed to close four of our stores and cut our workforce substantially. I remember thinking that during Gracyn's health crisis, nobody expected anything of me because there was nothing I could do. Yet in this business crisis, many were counting on me as the CEO to do something to save our business. The gravity of this reality weighed heavily on my heart and mind.

Just then, my wife, Robin, walked by and said, "Wow, don't you look like a depressed doofus! What could possibly be that bad?" Before I could respond, she lifted my chin and said, "Look at me. Remember when the doctors said there was nothing they could do for Gracyn? Remember every heart-breaking moment of helplessness we endured? What did we do? We trusted God and accepted His plan as perfect. Don't you think He would like you to do the same with the business? Place it in God's hands and trust Him, just like we did with Gracyn."

You would think someone who had just witnessed God's lifesaving work would not forget so quickly what to do. I guess I truly was a depressed doofus! Thankfully, Robin's lighthearted reminder led me to cast my burdens on God and trust Him, regardless of the current circumstance.

Relinquishing control to Him does not shirk our responsibly in any way; rather, it realigns us with the One who controls all things in our lives. I needed to pause and take a few deep breaths, breathing out the fear of "I can't" and breathing in the faith of "He can."

As our leadership team pondered these looming decisions, we collectively agreed on turning to God and trusting in Him, regardless of the potential outcome. We determined we would remain steadfast, navigate by our values, and persistently pursue our vision to SHINE, regardless of the situation. We prayed through every decision and asked God to bless each employee and family member who would be impacted by our decisions.

*"In the fear of the Lord there is strong confidence, and His children will have a place of refuge. The fear of the Lord is a fountain of life, to turn one away from the snares of death"* (Prov. 14:26–27, NKJV). Despite the economic chaos, our values steadied us with the confidence we needed to weather this and any other storm that may come our way. When we breathe in faith and breath out fear, confidence is produced.

# SET THE STANDARD

Years ago, when we first rolled out our corporate values, the immediate results were not pretty. Some unsettling issues began to surface in our organization. Employees who had prior witnessed questionable behavior without reporting it found new confidence to call out activities that were contradictory to our values. In one instance, we discovered a salesperson had been providing equipment at below-market prices to a company in which he was an unnamed business partner. He was secretly competing with other customers he was hired to serve. We also found that a few employees had been selling items for cash, pocketing the proceeds, and writing off the inventory as lost. Other inappropriate activities, which were previously unknown, began to surface.

Initially, learning of these improprieties was extremely disheartening. Yet in time, we understood that our values were filtering out the beliefs and behaviors that did not belong in our organization. Our values helped set the standards for how our organization should operate. Our values began to purify our organization by weeding out the attitudes and behaviors that could no longer be tolerated.

# BUILD FROM A FIRM FOUNDATION

As our company grew, we found that our values and vision attracted like-minded individuals who shared our ideals and wanted to join our team. As we continue to expand, it is our values and vision that bring us the right people for sustaining growth. I have discovered that the best source of employee recruitment is found in establishing godly values and then praying that the Lord will provide the right people. We pray He will send us the right employees to live out our values and pursue our vision. When we build our team on godly values, we establish a firm foundation. Jesus said this:

*Anyone who listens to My teaching and obeys it is wise, like a person who builds a house on solid rock. Though the rain comes in torrents and the floodwaters rise and the winds beat against that house, it won't collapse because it is built on bedrock.*

—Matthew 7:24, NLT

Our company has experienced some impressive growth over the years. We have greatly exceeded my expectations and grown beyond what I ever thought possible. As critical as our values were during the storms of turmoil, they are equally important as we experience continued growth and success. Without staying firmly grounded in Christ-like values, the trappings of success could divert us from our vision. Worldly values—such as wealth, pride, and power—could push us off course and direct us toward selfishness, rather than godliness. Regardless of what is going on around us, values establish a solid foundation of character that cannot be shaken. It is from this foundation that our confidence rises, allowing us to stand firm in our values, despite any circumstance, good or bad.

# SECURE STABILITY

Life typically comes at us at a fast pace. Every day, we face new challenges at work and in life. Adversity, temptation, and uncertainty lie in wait around every corner. Moral and ethical choices mark the roadways of our journey. In business, the winds of change are blowing continually. For a business to endure, it must navigate its way through the peaks and valleys of time and constant change. The founder of Walmart, Sam Walton, once said, "You can't just keep doing what works one time, because everything around you is always changing. To succeed, you have to stay out in front of that change."[1]

- Strategies change.

- Markets change.

- Economies change.

- Organizational structures change.

- Employees change.

- Managements change.

- Goals and objectives change.

- Compensation programs change.

- Customers change.

- Products change.

- Threats change.

Change is constant. It almost always brings discomfort. However, with change comes great opportunity. With everything changing all around us, great confidence can be found in navigating by core values that never change. When change comes your way, do not get wrapped up in worrying about all the things you cannot control. Think about

1. Sam Walton, *Made in America*, (New York: Doubleday, 1992), 249.

a small and tight circle of things you *can* do to make an impact, and block everything else out. Give everything outside your control to God, and then ask Him to help you with the things you can control. Stay within your circle of influence, and focus on things you can do that will make a difference. A company grounded in godly values finds confidence that allows change to strengthen and improve the organization.

· · · · · · · · · · · · · · · · · · · · · · · · · · · · · · · · · · · · · · · · · · ·

## *Change is constant. With change comes great opportunity.*

· · · · · · · · · · · · · · · · · · · · · · · · · · · · · · · · · · · · · · · · · · ·

Any employee who navigates by personal and operational values holds a distinct advantage in coping with change. Navigating by values instills the attitude of confidence. Trusting in godly values develops godly character, which leads to a life of integrity. Integrity builds the confidence to navigate through the storms of change and to come out better on the other side.

· · · · · · · · · · · · · · · · · · · · · · · · · · · · · · · · · · · · · · · · · · ·

## *Values Lead to Integrity*

· · · · · · · · · · · · · · · · · · · · · · · · · · · · · · · · · · · · · · · · · · ·

Confidence grows from a firm foundation anchored on values. When we trust our values and live them out, integrity is the result. Integrity happens when our beliefs, behaviors, and actions all line up. As Christ followers, it is our belief in Jesus that sets the course for our life's journey. Accepting the salvation of Christ makes heaven our eternal destination. Yet it is our behavior and actions that allow us to represent His Kingdom on the earth.

Think about it: Do your life actions represent His Kingdom? Do your beliefs and behaviors line up with godly values? When our beliefs and behaviors are rooted in Christ-like values, we can stand firm in the confidence that leads to our destiny. As Rick Warren said in *The Purpose Driven Life,* "Jesus did not die on the cross just so we could live comfortable, well-adjusted lives. His purpose is far deeper: He wants to make us like himself before he takes us to heaven. This is our greatest privilege, our immediate responsibility, and our ultimate destiny."[2]

We cannot reach our destiny of becoming like Christ on our own. It requires the Holy Spirit living in us and revealing His values through us. Just as a tree does not immediately produce fruit, neither do we immediately affect the world. A tree needs time to go through the process of becoming a fruit-bearer. Fruit is the product of what takes place in the growth of the tree. Likewise, as we grow in the Lord, His Spirit works in us so we can bear good fruit: *"The Holy Spirit produces this kind of fruit in our lives: love, joy, peace, patience, kindness, goodness, faithfulness, gentleness, and self-control..."* (Gal. 5:22–23, NLT).

It amazes me how little that sounds like me. It sure does sound an awful lot like Jesus, though. Does it not? Let us take a moment to

---

2. Warren, *The Purpose Driven Life*, 178.

consider the individual Fruit of the Spirit. How often do your actions reflect these values?

- Love
- Joy
- Peace
- Patience
- Kindness
- Goodness
- Gentleness
- Self-control

Over time, God uses the circumstances of our lives to develop our character. The more we place our confidence in Him, the more we begin to look like Christ. The power of His Spirit enables us to do what we cannot do alone: bear good fruit that reveals His character. Christ-like character is revealed when we allow His Spirit to work in us to produce His fruit.

So where—or in whom—should you place your confidence?

- Place your confidence in wealth, and you will be left empty.
- Place your confidence in power, and you will be left alone.
- Place your confidence in others, and you will be disappointed.
- Place your confidence in yourself, and you will be confused.
- Place your confidence in your feelings, and you will be wrong.
- Place your confidence in God's truth, and you will be secure.

Therefore, set the standard, lay the foundation, and secure stability. Place your confidence in God's values, and you will shine.

# NAVIGATE BY VALUES

Clarity—Know Your Values

Conviction—Live Your Values

Confidence—Trust Your Values

*The strength of integrity rises on Godly values.*

# EXCEL IN RELATIONSHIPS

*A new command I give you: Love one another.*
*As I have loved you, so you must love one another.*
*By this all men will know that you are My disciples,*
*if you love one another.*

—JOHN 13:34–35

## CHAPTER 17

# Ignite the Flame of Relationships

*Love your neighbor as yourself.*

—Matthew 22:39

Cable East, Inc., is a highly regarded communications contractor based in northeast Georgia. Founded in 1993, the company's goals have been to provide quality service at a fair price and to be the best, not the biggest. Cable East is known for its commitment, experience, and integrity. Over time, the company has become one of our most loyal customers. Owner Robert Wall explains:

> *It all started years ago when I was buying strictly from your competition. Vermeer Southeast had a salesman named Glenn who consistently stopped by to see me and check on how we were doing. I never actually purchased anything from Glenn, but he kept showing up, regardless. It was Glenn's perseverance and care for my company that eventually led me to give Vermeer a try. I am glad that Glenn is now one of your sales managers.*

*We've had our fair share of equipment problems along the way, but it was through these trials that Vermeer Southeast has proven to be worthy of my trust. As I would meet more people in the organization, I was impressed with how they all seemed to care about me as a customer and were always willing to do whatever they could to serve my needs. It amazed me that each person I would meet reminded me of Glenn. They knew what they were doing and would always ask, "How can I serve you better?" I remember thinking, "Where in the world do they find these people?"*

*My current sales representative, Bryan, is the same way. He is credible. I can count on him, and I know he cares. When Bryan gave me the book SHINE, it all made sense. Vermeer Southeast employees are this way because it is a part of their plan. They are motivated by a biblical vision that goes beyond just doing business. Personally, that means a lot to me. Quality products and a fair price are important; however, when it comes down to it, character is what matters most to me. It is all about the relationship. I know that I can count on Vermeer Southeast, and they know they can count on me. It is a great partnership. I have recommended them to many others over the years.*

# MAKING A SALE VS. MAKING A DIFFERENCE

In our business, it is easy to get all wrapped up in making sales and growing revenue. We strategically set sales goals and measure ourselves against these benchmarks. Sales and revenues are extremely important aspects of our business. Yet we need to be careful not to make them our primary motivation. We are not given work strictly for our own benefit. Rather, our work is given as an opportunity to meet with others and establish mutually beneficial relationships with them. When it is all said and done, nobody will care about how much we sold or how successful we were. It will be the relationships we have built along the way that truly will make a difference.

Our work should focus on making a friend before making a sale and making a difference before making a profit. It is not just about business. It is about building relationships, bringing value, and positively impacting the lives of others.

· · · · · · · · · · · · · · · · · · · · · · · · · · · · · · · · · · · · · · · · · ·

*Our work should focus on making a friend...not just a profit.*

· · · · · · · · · · · · · · · · · · · · · · · · · · · · · · · · · · · · · · · · · ·

This section, "Principle Five: Excel in Relationships," focuses on why we work, and it is slightly different than the other sections. The first four sections of the book focus on actions to be taken, whereas this section deals with the reason for those actions:

- When we serve others, honor God, improve continually, and navigate by values, the result is that we will excel in relationships.

- Loyal relationships are the product of living out the first four principles of SHINE.

- When our actions reveal these principles, we build loyal relationships while finding great pleasure and reward in our work.

*Moreover, when God gives any man wealth and possessions,*
*and enables him to enjoy them, to accept his lot and be happy in his*
*work—this is a gift of God.*

—Ecclesiastes 5:19

# REFERRALS VS. RECOMMENDATIONS

Referrals are highly coveted in the business world. Referrals are valuable because they help develop more business. Personally, I do not care as much about referrals as I care about recommendations. You see, a referral falls short of a recommendation because of one important aspect: a relationship. You might refer someone you have only heard of. However, you will only recommend someone with whom you have a relationship. A recommendation is much stronger than a referral because it is personal. It goes beyond a suggestion, and it becomes an endorsement based on a favorable experience and relationship. Recommendations are critical to the ongoing success of any enterprise.

As an employee, what greater compliment could you receive than a recommendation? Think about it. What usually comes first: a recommendation or a sale, a recommendation or a promotion, a recommendation or a raise? When we earn recommendations, good things follow. And, because we have earned those good things, we can enjoy them even more. Rather than simply seeking referrals, we shine when we focus on building loyal relationships that earn recommendations. A focus on meeting needs, working together, and valuing each other builds loyal relationships that can last a lifetime.

# GREAT DEAL VS. GREAT RELATIONSHIP

In the business world, we often encounter stiff competition. Our competitors might have a better price, better marketing, and perhaps even a better product. However, they can never take away the relationships we build with others. A loyal relationship is worth far more than any feature, advantage, or benefit.

Sometimes when we lose a deal to one of our competitors, we will try to blame the price or the product as the reason we lost the sale. Yet in most cases, the true difference-maker is the strength of relationship between supplier and customer. Far too often, we focus on product, price, or procedure when we should focus primarily on people. When we center our attention on revenues and profits, it rarely leads to relationships. However, a focus on people and relationships typically leads to increasing revenues and continuing profits.

· · · · · · · · · · · · · · · · · · · · · · · · · · · · · · · · · · · · · · ·

*Focus on people rather than product, price, or procedure.*

· · · · · · · · · · · · · · · · · · · · · · · · · · · · · · · · · · · · · · ·

Occasionally, employees change jobs to make more money somewhere else. A talented young employee once left our organization for a better offer in a different industry. We were shocked and disappointed that this individual would leave our company for just a few more dollars somewhere else. Eventually, we learned that the real reason this employee left was due to a strained relationship with his immediate supervisor.

In reality, the main reason most employees leave an organization is not because of dollars but because of relationships. I have heard that more than 70 percent of employees who change jobs do so because they do not feel valued by the company they left. When relationships are strong, an employee tends to stay:

- The employee feels valued.
- The employee's work is more rewarding.
- The employee's job satisfaction soars.

Leadership author John Maxwell says, "People respect a leader who keeps their interests in mind. If your focus is on what you can put into people rather than what you can get out of them, they'll love and respect you—and these create a great foundation for building relationships."[1]

# RELIGION VS. RELATIONSHIP

People enjoy their work more when they have strong relationships. That is how God made us. He created us to enjoy relationships with one another. Indeed, the major difference between Christianity and all other religions is that Christianity is not about rituals and religious rules. It is about a relationship with Jesus Christ. It is through this relationship that we are empowered by the Holy Spirit to do good works that glorify our Father in heaven. It is this loving relationship with Christ that we are called to share with others.

I recall a conversation I had with Anner, one of our past sales representatives from Puerto Rico. I was pleasantly surprised when he decided to share with me a personal struggle he was facing. At one

---

1  Maxwell, *The 21 Indispensable Qualities of a Leader*, 108.

point, I asked, "Is your heart right with God?"

"No, boss. No, it is not," he responded dejectedly. "My heart is very dark right now. Every day as I drive home from work, I drive past three churches, but I never go in. I know I should go to church. But I don't know which one to go to."

"It's not about going to church, Anner. The only way to get your heart right is through the love of Jesus," I shared as I looked him in the eyes.

His head stooped as he looked back at the ground.

"Let Jesus into your heart, and He will direct you which church to go to," I continued.

Lifting his head, Anner looked up at me and said, "Boss, don't look at me like that. You'll make me cry." As he walked away, he repeated, "Please don't look at me like that."

That is where our brief conversation ended that day. I felt as though I had let Anner down. I remember asking the Lord to touch Anner's heart and send someone who would do a better job of witnessing to him than I had.

Weeks later, I received this email message from Anner:

*I just want you to know that finally I know what it feels like to be with God. I went into church on Sunday, and my body started to sweat. It did not stop for nearly two hours till finally I found what I need. Others have been telling me that, and I'm sorry for not listening sooner. Now I know what that look you gave me is. That is the look of having peace in your heart. Other Christians have that same look. Now I have that look, too. Thank you, Kris, for giving me that look.*

Clearly "that look" has nothing to do with me. I am not capable of giving any human being a look that could make such an impact. Only the Holy Spirit can do that. In this case, my words had fallen short. The real reason I just stood there looking at Anner was that I did not know what else to say! God did not choose to work through my words that day. Instead, He chose to open Anner's eyes to see a relationship with Christ shining through my eyes.

# THE GREAT COMMISSION REVEALS SHINE

In the Great Commission, Jesus calls all believers to share this relationship with others:

> *Therefore, go and make disciples of all the nations, baptizing them in the name of the Father and the Son and the Holy Spirit.*
> *Teach these new disciples to obey all the commands I have given you. And be sure of this: I am with you always, even to the end of the age.*
> —Matthew 28:19–20, NLT

Note that all aspects of the Great Commission revolve around ongoing relationships. The Great Commission calls us to build loyal relationships with others, bring them to a relationship with God, grow together in discipleship, and walk together in fellowship and obedience—all of which flow from the loving relationship of our God living in us.

**S—Serve others.**

*"Go and make disciples of all the nations..."* (Matt. 28:19a).

**H—Honor God.**

*"...Baptizing them in the name of the Father and the Son and the Holy Spirit"* (Matt. 28:19b).

## I — Improve continually.

*"Teach these new disciples..."* (Matt. 28:20a).

## N — Navigate by values.

*"To obey all the commands I have given you"* (Matt. 28: 20b).

## E — Excel in relationships.

*"And be sure of this: I am with you always, even to the end of the age"* (Matt. 28:20c).

The most effective way to share our relationship in Christ is by building relationships with others. Loyal relationships are built on positive responses to the following questions:

- Can I trust you?
- Can I count on you?
- Do you care about me?

The answers to these questions reveal a lot about a person. From a work viewpoint, employees who can be trusted, who can be counted on, and who care about others will always earn recommendations. Better still, when our lives reveal *credibility*, *perseverance*, and *love*, we excel in relationships that can make an eternal impact.

## CHAPTER 18

# Shine with Credibility

## CAN I TRUST YOU?

*Do your best to present yourself to God as one approved,*
*a workman who does not need to be ashamed and*
*who correctly handles the word of truth.*

—2 Timothy 2:15

Shortly after revealing the SHINE message to me, the Lord began prompting me to share it with others. At that time in my life, doing so was way outside my comfort zone. I did not feel qualified or worthy to share a message from God with anyone. I took the safe approach, sharing it first with family, then with close friends, and eventually with our employees.

Not long afterward, I found myself in one of the most intimidating environments in which to share one's testimony: a roomful of my peers. I was addressing this group as I wrapped up a two-year term of serving as the president of our dealers' association. The room was filled with fellow equipment dealers, business managers, factory executives, key vendors, and their spouses for the banquet at our annual meeting. As the program drew to a close, the time came for me to pass the gavel to the incoming president. As I began to do so, I took an extended and somewhat awkward pause. A hush came over the room as I, contemplating my next move, stood silently. I could feel the Lord's prompting, but at the same time, I felt a sense of shame and trepidation.

Some of these people had known me for my entire career. They had known the cocky young kid who cared more about playing golf and having a good time than anything else. They surely would remember the insecure attention-craver who had often gone too far trying to prove his worthiness. There I stood, feeling wholly unworthy of sharing my testimony. The safe move would be to introduce the new president and quietly take my seat.

Suddenly the words, "Before I sit down, I have one more thing to share with you" came out of my mouth. There was no turning back now—every eye in the room was focused on me.

"A few years ago, I realized how inconsistent my life was. I was living one life at work, another life at home, and still another at church on the weekend," I said. "Then, in one of those defining moments, spent alone with my Creator, God revealed a profound truth: I have been given only one life to live, and I need to live it wholly committed to honoring God in all that I do."

I professed Jesus as the Light in my life, walked them through the principles of SHINE, and then encouraged them to seek the same. Finally, I passed the gavel to our new president and sat down.

I noticed tears in my wife's eyes as she mouthed the words, "I am proud of you." Looking up, I was surprised to see the entire audience on their feet and applauding. It was at that moment that I fully grasped the SHINE vision. I recalled wondering some time earlier, "Would anyone ever applaud me for the work I do?" The Lord had answered that question with a Scripture passage.

Now it all made sense. We are indeed called to SHINE—to stand out in a way that others would take notice—not for our own applause, but for the good works He does in and through us. Whether the crowd understood it or not, I knew their applause was not for me. Their praise and appreciation was not given for any good work of mine, but for the glory of my Father in heaven. Jesus had given me the credibility to shine.

> *Let your light so shine before men, that they may see your good works and glorify your Father in heaven.*
> —Matthew 5:16, NKJV

# DO WHAT YOU SAY

The first mark of credibility is established when we live up to our promises. It is revealed when our actions match our words. It is found in doing what we say we will do. Credibility rises on the firm foundation of honesty and responsibility. Personal résumés, for example, can lack credibility. Employers, how often have you looked back at someone's résumé and wished that the employee you hired would live up to what his or her résumé says? Often on a résumé or in job interview, people try to make themselves look better than they really are. When this is the case, the entire employment process begins with a lack of credibility. It's doomed before it even gets started.

Employees (or job seekers), let me encourage you to closely read over your latest résumé. Does it adequately describe who you are and what you do? Or is it designed to make you look better than what your track record proves? If it is the latter, you have a choice: you can change your resumé and lower it to your actual performance, or you can improve your performance and start doing what your résumé says you will do. That is credibility.

Employers, do you provide everything that you have promised to your employees? How about to your customers? Does your business seek to live up to its own hype?

. . . . . . . . . . . . . . . . . . . . . . . . . . . . . . . . . . . . . . .

*Christianity and credibility should be*

*one and the same.*

. . . . . . . . . . . . . . . . . . . . . . . . . . . . . . . . . . . . . . .

*Credibility* results when you do what you say you will do, and it is living up to who you say you are. Scripture exhorts us, *"Be an example to all believers in what you say, in the way you live, in your love, your faith, and your purity"* (1 Tim. 4:12, NLT).

# DO WHAT IS RIGHT

Christianity and credibility should be one and the same. As Christ's followers, it is His credibility that should guide us in life and work. Credibility reveals itself over time as we represent Christ in our daily walk. Credible employers pay bills on time and live up to every obligation. Credible workers get things done. They do not make excuses but come through by meeting and exceeding expectations.

They are prompt, they meet deadlines, and they can be counted on at all times. They do not take shortcuts or skimp on quality. They do not grumble and complain. Rather, they display an eagerness to model Christ with positive words and actions. They do not bow to emotions or make decisions based on popularity.

> *Obviously, I'm not trying to win the approval of people, but of God. If pleasing people were my goal, I would not be Christ's servant.*
> —Galatians 1:10, NLT

Credible decisions are based on choosing what is right over what is popular. Credibility is standing for beliefs and ideals in all circumstances by choosing God's way, especially when the pressure is on. Serving Christ by working for Him might not always be popular, but it is always right. At work, Christians reveal credibility when their work reflects a witness for Jesus Christ. Pastor and author Charles Swindoll says, "The very best platform upon which we may build a case for Christianity at work rests on six massive pillars: integrity, faithfulness, punctuality, quality workmanship, a pleasant attitude, and enthusiasm. Hire such a person and it will be only a matter of time before business will improve…people will be impressed… and Christianity will begin to seem important."[1]

Credibility is clearly found in God's Word. Adhering to it yields a bountiful return: *"And the seeds that fell on the good soil represent honest, good-hearted people who hear God's word, cling to it, and patiently produce a huge harvest"* (Luke 8:15, NLT). The seed is always good because it is the Word of truth. Only the soil in which it germinates differs. The soil of our character determines the harvest we produce. Through the credibility of God's Word, we produce a

---

1. Charles Swindoll, *Growing Strong in the Seasons of Life* (Portland, OR: Multnomah Press, 1983), 58.

crop beyond our wildest dreams that produces good works glorifying our Father in heaven.

# DO IT WELL

Credibility is also built when you do your job well. The more knowledgeable you become in your field of endeavor, the more credible you become. Remember, regardless of your position at work, credibility can help shape culture and make others around you better.

- Strive to become an expert who knows your work well.

- Strive to become the type of person others seek out for answers to their questions.

- Strive to become someone who always performs with excellence.

- Strive to become an encourager who always focuses on relationships.

- Strive to be a go-to person others can count on.

Shortly after becoming CEO of our company, an intriguing résumé crossed my desk. It was one of those mass-mail types—from an outplacing firm—that typically ended up in my garbage can. But for some reason, I could not toss this one out. I discussed this candidate's qualifications with our team. These are some responses I recall: "Why would he want to work here? He is way overqualified for our company." "This guy should be the president of a bank or some large financial institution." "This looks like a great candidate—if you want to hire your boss."

Even though Jon was clearly overqualified, we made him an offer to become our CFO. I have to admit, it was somewhat intimidating to hire someone who, based on his résumé, could be my boss. Yet looking back, it is one of the best decisions we ever made at Vermeer Southeast. Jon has become that "go-to person" in our organization. Everyone knows they can count on Jon to get the job done and provide sound advice. Jon's expertise and work ethic have helped fuel responsible growth in our organization. His integrity has helped build trusting relationships with banks, lenders, and other critical providers. Most importantly, Jon's character and consistency have helped shape the culture of our organization. Jon's credibility shines through in all he does. The moral of this story: don't be afraid to hire someone who could be your boss. It could be God's way of enhancing your own credibility. When we are surrounded by others with credibility, we, too, become more credible.

## SHINE REVEALS CREDIBILITY

Credibility draws the attention of others. People respect, listen to, and trust those who have proven their credibility. Loyal relationships are founded on the strength of credibility. When Christ shines in us, credibility is a result.

**S–Serve others.** A heart of servanthood glorifies God by helping others. Humility is putting others first. One of the quickest ways to lose credibility is through a selfish attitude. Conversely, when our motives are focused on others rather than on ourselves, we gain credibility. Build credibility by serving others.

**H–Honor God.** A soul of faithfulness obeys God's purpose. Trust is depending on Him. By trusting in God, obeying His Word, and leaving our outcomes to Him, we earn the trust of those around us. Build credibility by honoring God.

**I–Improve continually.** A mind of excellence pursues God's vision. Competence is soaring with our strengths. When we pursue

God's vision, we grow toward becoming all that God created us to be. Competence breeds credibility. Build credibility by improving continually.

**N–Navigate by values.** The strength of integrity rises on godly values. Clarity is found in knowing our values. Clear values help us to make clear decisions personally, professionally, and corporately. Values of integrity keep us on the right track and reveal credibility. Build credibility by navigating according to your values.

**E–Excel in relationships.** Loyal relationships flow from God's love. Credibility is revealed through humility, trust, competence, and clarity. Credibility develops loyal relationships by positively answering the question, "Can I trust you?"

**CHAPTER 19**

# Shine with Perseverance

CAN I COUNT ON YOU?

*Consider it pure joy my brothers whenever you face trials of many kinds, because you know that the testing of your faith develops perseverance. Perseverance must finish its work so that you may be mature and complete, not lacking anything.*

—James 1:2–4

During the coronavirus pandemic of 2020, we were participating in a conference call with our regional managers when someone remarked, "I don't know why, but we seem to be at our best when times get the toughest." As our discussion continued, some answers were revealed about why that is true.

"How do we want to be remembered when this is over? What do we want customers, fellow employees, and our families to say about how we handled this situation?" one RM asked.

"This is our moment to shine. Many people will be watching us," another added. "Let's be that positive influence on all of those whom we come in contact with. This is our opportunity to go beyond work, ask about families, and show how much we care beyond just business."

"We need to take this opportunity for training and to get better at what we do. When things are slow, it's the best time to grow!" another said.

"We need to be thankful in the midst of this pandemic," reflected yet another. "There will be so much bad news floating around. Let's remain positive and bring the good news. Remember, we may be the only light some people get to see."

Let's face it. The longer we walk the earth the more experience we will gain in dealing with trials. Downturns, financial losses, hurricanes, storms, health scares, family emergencies…the list goes on and on. We all face trials and storms in this life. The secret lies in where we turn in times of crisis and how we navigate through these challenges.

*And let us run with perseverance the race marked out for us,*
*fixing our eyes on Jesus, the pioneer and perfector of faith.*
—Hebrews 12:1–2

After my daughter's heart transplant and in the midst of the 2008–10 business draught, we published a pocket-sized booklet called *Crisis Survival Guide*. It includes Scripture, prayers, and coping skills required to deal with a crisis. One of the most important lessons in the booklet deals with where we turn in times of crisis:

## Why vs. What

When crisis happens we often find ourselves asking, "Why? Why did this happen to me?"

A better question is, What? What can I learn from this? What should I be praying right now?"

## When vs. Work

When crises happen, we often find ourselves asking, "When? When will this crisis end? When will life get back to normal?"

It is better to remember that God has a plan. If you find yourself wanting to ask, "When?" this is the perfect time to simply ask God to work His plan and to trust Him with the outcome.

## Worry vs. Worship

When crises happen, we often find ourselves overtaken by worry. During a crisis, it is natural to worry.

A better response is to turn to God and worship Him in times of worry. Turn your worry over to Him, and ask Him to guide you. Thank Him for being in control. We worship Him when we thank Him and express our trust in Him.

*Why, when, and worry* reveal a focus on ourselves and the situations we face. *What, work, and worship* take the focus off our crises and turn our focus to God.

> *We don't know what to do but our eyes are on you.*
> —2 Chronicles 20:12

> *Take up your positions, stand firm and see the deliverance the Lord will give you. Do not be afraid; do not be discouraged. Go out to face them tomorrow, and the Lord will be with you.*
> —2 Chronicles 20:17

Are you facing difficulty? Do you find yourself in the midst of crisis? Turn to the One on whom you can count. Reflect on the preceding scriptural passages that provide a prescription for perseverance.

- Take your position.
- Stand firm.
- See the deliverance the Lord will give you.
- Do not be afraid.
- Do not be discouraged.
- Go out to face your challenges and adversaries.
- The Lord will be with you.

# PRESS ON

God is preparing us for something great, something beyond what we could ever hope for or imagine. Crowns, mansions, and heavenly treasures await those who place their trust in Him. By His grace, our future is set. But let us not forgo today. Too many believers are so focused on tomorrow that they miss the opportunity to represent His Kingdom right here and now. Our work is a means to represent the Kingdom of God. Let us not ever forget our responsibility to SHINE every day in the works we do as we represent Him, both now and forever.

In *A Life God Rewards*, Bruce Wilkinson says there is a direct connection between what we do on earth and what God will do for us in heaven: "Simple decisions, such as how you spend your time and money, will become opportunities of great promise. And you will begin to live with an unshakable certainty that everything you do today matters forever."[1]

---

1. Bruce Wilkinson, *A Life God Rewards* (Sisters, OR: Multnomah Publishers, 2002), 16.

......................................

*We are called to press on.*

......................................

Never forget: when we accept Christ as Lord, we immediately become a part of His Kingdom. It is not just a future Kingdom, but one that is very present and very real—right where we are. His Kingdom is present and thriving today in our families, our workplaces, and the world around us. The things we do now to represent our eternal King are preparing us for our everlasting future. We are called to persevere and to press on as God advances His Kingdom through us for all eternity.

## STAND FIRM IN TRIALS

Everything we hear and imagine about heaven and God's eternal Kingdom seems so perfect. In contrast, our daily lives can be filled with so many challenges and difficulties. Around each corner of our journey lies countless problems, trials, and setbacks. Life at work is no different. Choosing to seek a work life that shines does not mean everything will be easy. Trials will come our way at work, in spite of our commitment to His Kingdom and, sometimes, because of our commitment to SHINE.

We often will stumble and make mistakes. I would hate to admit how often I have been discouraged as our company and I have fallen short of our vision to SHINE with excellence. Some days, it appears that we do the exact opposite of our vision. Other days, it seems like problem after problem is stacking up against us. We often fail to adequately represent our vision. Yet we are called to persevere.

We cannot avoid trials, failures, and problems; however, we can choose our response to them. We can decide to be consumed by problems. We can cut and run from them. We can shut down and be defeated by our failures. On the other hand, we can choose to trust God to mature us, complete us, and direct us to persevere through and overcome the trials we face. We can rise up and move on, not defeated by our failures but inspired to grow from them. Learning to endure and overcome is an undeniable requirement of God's plan for those who represent His Kingdom.

*We can rejoice, too, when we run into problems and trials, for we know that they help us develop endurance. And endurance develops strength of character, and character strengthens our confident hope of salvation.*

—Romans 5:3–4, NLT

When we rejoice in our salvation, our problems have a tendency to look much smaller. Great perseverance is found in knowing that God always fulfills His promises. When we trust Him, He uses trials to strengthen our resolve, our character, and our relationship with Him.

## NEVER GIVE UP

A great story of perseverance—of never giving up—comes from one of our top sales representatives. He had been trying for months to get the president of a power company to look at one of our new pieces of equipment. The problem was that this particular customer had experienced problems with one of our machines many years prior and had no intention of considering us for this upcoming purchase. Our representative diligently pursued this opportunity with phone calls, personal visits, apologies, pleadings, and whatever else—all to no avail. The customer simply refused to even look at our equipment.

Upon hearing that the company had given a verbal order to our competition for a new piece of equipment, our sales representative decided to try one more thing. He got up really early, picked up a new machine, and parked it in the president's reserved parking space. "I have nothing to lose in forcing him to look at it," he reasoned. It was through this confident act of perseverance that our sales representative received his audience with the president. And, yes, the story has a happy ending.

The customer cancelled his order with the competitor and purchased the machine from us. The reason? This customer realized that he could count on our employee to persevere, regardless of the challenge, and to be there for him. To top it all off—years later—this sales representative became the president of our company. As Scott will attest, perseverance can indeed pay great dividends.

## FIGHT THE GOOD FIGHT

*Perseverance* is steady, continuous belief and action despite ongoing difficulty or setbacks. Those who choose to persevere do not turn and run when things get tough. Rather, they resolve to endure challenging situations. Those who consistently persevere show they are trustworthy in their actions, which often results in their earning recommendations for their diligence and reliability.

Are you facing any trials in your life or work right now? List your biggest challenges here:

_____

_____

_____

_____

_____

_____

_____

_____

It is in times of struggle, like those you currently are facing, that you can receive great blessing. Make the choice to persevere with God's help. Give these challenges to God, and ask Him to carry you through. You can learn and grow through trials in ways you never could when times are easy. These experiences afford you the opportunity to deepen your relationship with God and to build and grow relationships with others.

Perseverance allows us to continue moving toward God's promise. His promise provides hope and a future. It inspires us to give our best, regardless of how we feel and the situations around us.

Scripture encourages us to make every effort to press on and keep the faith. God's promise provides believers with a favorable eternal outcome for each of our life stories. What truly matters in the big picture is our relationship with Him. For those who remain faithful to that relationship and finish strong, the prize for perseverance awaits.

*I have fought a good fight, I have finished the race, and I have remained faithful. And now the prize awaits me—the crown of righteousness, which the Lord, the righteous Judge, will give me on the day of his return. And the prize is not just for me but for all who eagerly look forward to his appearing*

—2 Timothy 4:7–8, NLT

# SHINE REVEALS PERSEVERANCE

Perseverance is a greatly admired characteristic that captures people's attention. We all love to hear stories of continued perseverance that culminate with great reward in the end. Through Christ, our own perseverance will lead to a life story concluding with great reward. When Christ shines in us, perseverance is a result.

**S—Serve others.** A heart of servanthood glorifies God by helping others. Generosity is exceeding expectations. By going the extra mile, serving the Lord heartily, and working with great enthusiasm, we develop the momentum needed to keep moving ahead toward God's promise. Develop perseverance by serving others.

**H—Honor God.** A soul of faithfulness obeys God's purpose. Stewardship is serving Him. By yielding to Him, placing our priority on Him, and taking the perspective that He is in control, we become empowered by Him. Develop perseverance by honoring God.

**I—Improve continually.** A mind of excellence pursues God's vision. Courage is taking action. By facing our fears, looking ahead, and taking action, we overcome the roadblocks that mark our path. Develop perseverance by improving continually.

**N—Navigate by values.** The strength of integrity rises on godly values. Confidence is found in trusting our values. Confidence inspires us to fight the good fight, finish the race, and run to win. Develop perseverance while navigating by values.

**E—Excel in relationships.** Loyal relationships flow from God's love. Perseverance is revealed through generosity, stewardship, courage, and confidence. When we exceed expectations, serve Him, take action, and trust our values, perseverance is produced. Build perseverance by excelling in relationships. Perseverance develops loyal relationships by answering the question, "Can I count on you?"

## CHAPTER 20

# Shine with Love

## DO YOU CARE ABOUT ME?

*If I gave everything I have to the poor and even sacrificed my body, I could boast about it; but if I didn't love others, I would have gained nothing.*

— 1 Corinthians 13:3, NLT

Acquisitions can be a strategic way to grow a business and fortify a team. Our acquisition of sales territories in Alabama and the Florida panhandle accomplished both. It also allowed us to lure back a top employee who had previously left our company. Scott had a great job and was not looking to leave his current job when I approached him about running our new acquisition. Although his initial response was no, he said he was open to praying about it.

Eventually, Scott informed me, "Where I am now, I can accomplish all my personal and professional goals. But I feel if I return to Vermeer Southeast, I will be able to impact people for eternity. When it comes down to it, I really want my work to count for eternity."

With a proven leader on board, the deal was closed, and the transition began. Revenues proved higher than expected, and we were thrilled with the new employees we gained. Most were excited about joining our company, except for one employee: the prior owner's son-in-law, Mickey. While he was cordial, it was obvious he was not buying in to what we were saying.

Normally, revenue growth, employee retention, and profitability would have been the most valuable rewards of a successful business acquisition, but this one was different. During Scott's annual review, I asked him what he was most proud of in his first year of running the new business. His answer took me by surprise. He smiled and said, "Mickey."

Scott shared that Mickey had always envisioned himself owning the dealership. Our purchase had taken away his dream. When we came in with our new plans and shared our SHINE vision, he did not want any part of it. Mickey's expertise in a certain line of our equipment allowed him to travel around to our various locations to help out. Over time, he began to see that the SHINE vision was more than just words. Everywhere he went, our people were good to him. They treated him with respect and made him feel like a valuable member of the team.

Once, while working with one of our salespeople, Mickey shared a difficult situation he was facing. Our sales rep asked if he could pray for him. Mickey was shocked that someone would pray for him at work.

A few days later, Mickey accepted Jesus Christ as his Savior. Mickey told Scott, "Now I know why you guys got to buy this business, instead of me. I would have never been saved in a church or anywhere else, for that matter. The only place I could have come to Christ is at work. You guys showed me how cool it is to be a Christian, even at work. Because of that, I have found Jesus." A few weeks later, another employee told Mickey about some personal struggles. Of course, Mickey did not hesitate to recommend Jesus Christ as the answer.

# LOVE GOD

God is at work all around us, building His Kingdom while reconciling a lost world. We can recommend Christ to others, but the truth is, only God can build His Kingdom. One of the most effective ways that God grows His Kingdom is through our relationships. We shine when God works in us to build eternal relationships that glorify Him.

· · · · · · · · · · · · · · · · · · · · · · · · · · · · · · · · · · · · · · · · ·

## *We shine when God works in us.*

· · · · · · · · · · · · · · · · · · · · · · · · · · · · · · · · · · · · · · · · ·

The apostle Paul wrote, *"Three things will last forever—faith, hope, and love—and the greatest of these is love"* (1 Corin. 13:13, NLT). No emotion or attitude is stronger than love. Love lasts forever. Love is the most important quality we can exemplify. It is the key to our relationship with God. In fact, God is most glorified in us when we love Him as Jesus commands: *"Love the Lord your God with all your heart and with all your soul and with all your mind and with all your strength"* (Mark 12:30).

# LOVE YOURSELF

Love is the key to all our relationships. Jesus said, *"Love your neighbor as yourself..."* (Mark 12:31). We often grasp the call to love our neighbors. Harder to fully grasp is Jesus's command for us to love ourselves. The love of self that Jesus refers to is not physical love, selfish love, or surface love. He is referring to spiritual love, the type of love that only God can provide. *"God is love. Whoever lives in love lives in God, and God in him"* (1 John 4:16).

When we accept Jesus as our Savior and confess Him as Lord of our lives, He sends His Spirit to live in us, and our salvation is secured. But that is where a new battle begins, At that point, the evil one changes tactics. He uses every tool in his arsenal to distract us and convince us that we are not measuring up, that we are unworthy of God's love. Our enemy's greatest desire is to keep us from living in the fullness of God's love. Yet God's greatest desire is for a loving relationship with us. If we love God, and He lives in us, how could we not appropriately love ourselves? True love for self is found in understanding that we are children of God. When we love and respect ourselves as children of God, we can then love and respect others as children of God as well.

# LOVE RELATIONSHIPS, NOT THINGS

"I love my job." "I hate my job." These two statements are clearly at opposite ends of the spectrum. Yet I submit they can be equally unhealthy statements. In either scenario, a more appropriate statement would be, "I love God, and I am thankful for the work He provides." If you hate your job, remember that God gave you work as a blessing and an opportunity to do good works that glorify Him. If you love your job, be careful not to make your work more important than your love for God and others. The demands and rewards of work can distract us from loving God and, if left unchecked, can diminish our love for those around us.

I would never intentionally put my love for work before my love for family. Yet often my behavior can lead to that exact perception.

Once, while my daughter was in the hospital, I spent all day watching shows and movies with her. As Robin "relieved me" so I could go do some business, I lingered outside and overheard a conversation between Robin and Gracyn. Robin asked, "How was your day?"

"It was great, Mom," Gracyn replied, "Dad's phone rang eleven times, and he didn't even answer it once."

This pierced my heart. My daughter was clinging to life in a pediatric intensive care unit, and most important to her that day was that her dad did not answer his cell phone when it rang. My prior actions had led my little girl to believe my work calls were more important than she was. The truth is, each of my children felt I had put my work before them. I asked for their forgiveness, and I asked God to help me do a better job of showing my love for them.

Years later, I was doing a devotional that required listing things for which I would die. I immediately wrote down my faith, my kids, and my wife. The point of the devotional was that relationships should be the most important treasures in our lives. As I closed my devotional time in prayer, I sensed the Lord prodding me to be honest. As much as I did not want to admit it, an honest answer would have been my faith, my kids, and my work. This was alarming.

For years, Robin had felt like she needed more love from me. She did not feel like I had prioritized our relationship. The truth is, next to our love for God, the marriage relationship should be our top priority. Yet it is common for many of us to allow our work to trump that relationship at times. That is not what God desires. There I was, seeking to run a business for God's glory, writing and speaking about it, yet going home to a wife who did not feel adequately loved by me. Again, I asked God for forgiveness and asked for His help. I asked Robin to forgive me, and together we asked God to overflow our hearts with love for God and each other.

Thankfully, God's grace is enough. I asked Him to break the chains binding my heart so I could love Robin and my family in the same way He loves me. I sense there are many children and spouses across the globe who are longing for the same. God gives us work as a blessing. He delights in excellent work that glorifies Him. Yet it is not a true reflection of His love if that work distracts us from adequately loving those closest to us. Only the sacrificial, selfless, unconditional love of God releases us from selfishness and frees us to love others in the same way. When we open ourselves to experience the fullness of God's love, He equips us to love others sufficiently as well.

# LOVE OTHERS

So, what does this love of self and others have to do with business? I am not suggesting that you ask your fellow employees to join hands Monday morning and sing *Kumbaya*. I am also not suggesting that you give every customer who walks through your door a big hug accompanied with tears of joy. (Although it might be kind of fun to see their reactions!) No, I am suggesting that you love God with all you have and love others as Scripture teaches:

> *Love is patient, love is kind. It does not envy, it does not boast, it is*

*not proud. It does not dishonor others, it is not self-seeking, it is not easily angered, it keeps no record of wrongs. Love does not delight in evil but rejoices with the truth. It always protects, always trusts, always hopes, always perseveres. Love never fails.*

—1 Corinthians 13:4–8

This kind of love sustains, empowers, and delights you. It will fill your heart to overflowing. The radiance of this love will draw others to you for developing new relationships. His love then connects others to Jesus Christ through you. The greatest recommendation of all—recommending Jesus—flows powerfully through love and builds loyal relationships that last forever. It is true that none of us can live a perfect life, but in Jesus Christ, we all can experience His perfect love.

*So that Christ may dwell in your hearts though faith. And I pray that you, being rooted and established in love, may have power, together with all the Lord's holy people to grasp how wide and long and high and deep is the love of Christ, and to know this love that surpasses all knowledge—that you may be filled to the measure of all the fullness of God.*

—Ephesians 3:17–19

*Love* develops loyal relationships by answering the question, "Do you care about me?"

## SHINE REVEALS LOVE

Nothing attracts the attention of others like God's love. We reveal our love for God by showing His love to others. Love is how an invisible God becomes visible. We shine when God's love is seen in us:

**S—Serve others.** A heart of servanthood glorifies God by helping others. *"You shall love the Lord your God with all your heart…"* (Mark 12:30). Humility, compassion, and generosity lead to an attitude of love. God has called each of us to a mission of service. We shine when God's love is seen in us.

**H—Honor God.** A soul of faithfulness obeys God's purpose. *"You shall love the Lord your God with all your… soul"* (Mark 12:30). Trust, gratitude, and stewardship lead to an attitude of love. When God works through us to accomplish His purposes, we reveal the soul of Christ. We shine when God's love is seen in us.

**I—Improve continually.** A mind of excellence pursues God's vision. *"You shall love the Lord your God with all your… mind"* (Mark 12:30). Competence, courage, and passion lead to an attitude of love. When we pursue God's vision, we reveal the mind of Christ. We shine when God's love is seen in us.

**N—Navigate by values.** The strength of integrity rises on godly values. *"You shall love the Lord your God with all your…strength"* (Mark 12:30). Clarity, conviction, and confidence lead to an attitude of love. Godly values reveal the strength of integrity found in Christ. We shine when God's love is seen in us.

**E—Excel in relationships.** Loyal relationships flow from God's love. *"You shall love your neighbor as yourself"* (Mark 12:31). Life is all about love. God is love, and He lives in those who love Him. We shine when God's love is seen in us.

*A new command I give you: Love one another. As I have loved you, so you must love one another. By this all men will know that you are My disciples, if you love one another.*

—John 13:34–35

So, how about you? Do others know you are a disciple of Christ by the way you love them? Take a moment to reflect on these questions. How would customers, fellow employees, friends, and family members respond if asked these questions about you?

- Can I trust you?

- Can I count on you?

- Do you care about me?

Now imagine if Jesus were to ask you these questions. What would your response be? What would your life show as answers to the questions?

- Can I trust you? (credibility)

- Can I count on you? (perseverance)

- Do you care about me? (love)

# EXCEL IN RELATIONSHIPS

Credibility—Can I trust you?

Perseverance—Can I count on you?

Love—Do you care about me?

*Loyal relationships flow from God's love.*

# SHINE On!

If you own or run a business, eventually you will need to pass your business and your responsibilities on to a successor. If you believe that God owns your business, do you have the right to sell it to the highest bidder and walk away? If you are navigating by Godly values, is it okay to pass it on to someone who may not share those values? What about the ministry that is done through your business? Is it acceptable for that to be discontinued? These are important questions for Christian business leaders as they consider succession-planning for their companies.

We recently transitioned our company to new owners. As we considered all options, it became clear that selling the shares of our company to our employees through an ESOP, (Employee Stock Ownership Plan), was the best way to transition Vermeer Southeast to the next generation of leaders.

If you look at the example of Jesus, an ESOP certainly makes some sense. Think about it. Jesus did not pick a successor, make him Christ, and then return to heaven. He certainly did not seek to find the highest bidder and then go do something else. No, instead, he hand-picked a team, mentored them, and empowered them to carry on the mission. Who better to carry on the mission of an organization than the very team that has been doing it for years?

I am not suggesting that an ESOP is the right transition tool for everyone. I am certainly not trying to compare myself to Jesus. But in our case, transitioning to an ESOP was the best way to ensure that the SHINE Vision would be carried forward into the future. I am confident that our leadership team—guided by our vision—will inspire our employee owners to shine for years to come.

The SHINE vision continually manifests itself through stories like you have just read and many others of which I will never hear. But, that is exactly how God works. We do not always know when it is happening. However, when God works in us, He makes eternal differences for His Kingdom. When Christ shines in us, His impact reaches beyond significance.

Over time, I have noticed four distinct stages through which we can pass in our careers.

## Stage 1: Survival

Stage one is when the sole justification for our work is to meet our own needs. At the survival stage, our work is a means to a paycheck and a way to get by. At this stage, our work typically has little meaning. Many spend entire careers at this stage, just putting in time. At the survival stage, workers usually perform to a minimal standard. Rarely is fulfillment found here. Survival is what we do to get by.

## Stage 2: Success

Stage two is the success stage. At this stage, motivation tends to be high. We see something we want, and we do whatever it takes to get it. Money, prestige, and accolades drive us to pursue victory at all costs. Some of the highest-achieving employees live at this stage. The success stage promotes personal gratification. Success is what we do for ourselves.

## Stage 3: Significance

Stage three is the significance stage, where work life can be highly rewarding. This stage produces workers with high internal motivation. Instead of focusing on individual achievement, they focus on helping others reach their goals. Teamwork and fulfillment run high at this stage. The significance stage is about promoting others and making an impact through them. Significance is what we do for others.

## Stage 4: SHINE

Stage four is the SHINE stage. When we shine, we need not worry about survival. When we shine, success is a given. When we shine, we significantly impact the lives of others. SHINE is not something we can do on our own. Shine is when God works in and through us.

Throughout our careers, we might find ourselves bouncing back and forth among these stages. However, regardless of what happens in life, the SHINE vision keeps our eyes on Jesus and always leads us back to the SHINE stage.

# LET GOD'S LIGHT SHINE

At the SHINE stage, where true fulfillment is found, Christ lives in us. He shines in us as we seek the following objectives and take the corresponding actions:

| | |
|---|---|
| God's mission | **Serve others** |
| God's purpose | **Honor God** |
| God's vision | **Improve continually** |
| God's values | **Navigate by values** |
| God's relationships | **Excel in relationships** |

When our focus is on God, and we depend fully on His Light, our future will always be bright. Still, there are times that we will not shine. The desires and distractions of life beckon from the darkness.

In the darkness, we chase our own dreams and make selfish decisions for our own benefit. Greed, guilt, pride, and other powers from the darkness conspire to bring us down. When we rely on our own power, our faith decreases and we drift away from the light. The darkness waits eagerly to engulf us. Yet, even in the depths of the darkness there is always hope.

*I am the light of the world. If you follow Me, you won't have to walk in darkness, because you will have the light that leads to life.*
—John 8:12, NLT

Darkness, by definition, is the absence of light. Jesus is the Light of the world. He dispels the darkness. The SHINE vision points to Jesus who lights the way. The more we rely on Him, the more transparent we become. In our own transparency, we no longer rely on ourselves, but on the Light of the world shining in us. Inspired by His vision and consumed by His presence, we rise from the darkness, and by the power of His light, we reflect His glory

> *You are the light of the world. A city that is set on a hill cannot be hidden. Nor do they light a lamp and put it under a basket, but on a lampstand, and it gives light to all who are in the house. Let your light so shine before men, that they may see your good works and glorify your Father in heaven.*
>
> —Matthew 5:14–16, NKJV

Jesus is the Light. We are His lampstands. We SHINE when His light is seen in us. In Him, we find meaning and purpose. Our work is no longer only about making a living. Rather, it is a way of living—of standing out like a city on a hill—where He allows us to SHINE for His glory.

SHINE on!

# ABOUT THE AUTHOR

Kris DenBesten currently serves as CEO of Vermeer Southeast, a construction equipment company headquartered in Orlando, Florida. Under his leadership, the company has experienced growth in annual sales to more than $150 million and has successfully transitioned to a 100 percent employee-owned ESOP organization.

Kris has written three books on leadership, facing crisis, and living by faith. He is a down-to-earth, from-the-heart communicator who effectively connects with all audiences. Kris shares his message of hope and Christ's empowerment as he encourages others to join in the marketplace ministry movement.

He and his wife, Robin, live in central Florida, and have three grown children: Cole, Gracyn, and Brooks.

Contact Kris DenBesten at **kris@shinevision.com.**

Visit **www.shinevision.com.**

# IF YOU'RE A FAN OF THIS BOOK, WILL YOU HELP ME SPREAD THE WORD?

There are several ways you can help me get the word out about the message of this book…

- Post a 5-Star review on Amazon.

- Write about the book on your Facebook, Twitter, Instagram, LinkedIn – any social media you regularly use!

- If you blog, consider referencing the book, or publishing an excerpt from the book with a link back to my website. You have my permission to do this as long as you provide proper credit and backlinks.

- Recommend the book to friends – word-of-mouth is still the most effective form of advertising.

- Purchase additional copies to give away as gifts.

**The best way to connect or buy additional copies is by visiting www.shinevision.com.**

# ENJOY THESE OTHER BOOKS
# BY KRIS DENBESTEN

### The Shine Factor

*Finding Significance in Life and Work*

Imagine reaching the end of your life journey and realizing much of your time and energy were focused on the wrong things. What would you change? How would you live differently if given another chance?

Meet Robert Elder, a performance driven high-achieving business owner. In this parable, take a ride with him on the highway to success. Prepare yourself for an unexpected detour that could make all the difference in your life.

### Gracyn's Song

*A Journey from Facing Crisis to Finding Hope*

Maybe you are facing an unspeakable tragedy or have a dark challenge looming on your horizon. Maybe you've already endured tragedy or find yourself fearing the unknown. Regardless, you will find hope and healing as you share in the DenBesten's journey of faith and apply the lessons they learned to your own situation.

### Crisis Survival Guide

This pocket-sized booklet includes 10 key survival lessons learned through Gracyn's medical crisis. It also contains applicable scripture, prayers and practical coping skills for anyone facing any crisis.

**Visit www.shinevision.com to order copies of these books and for additional resources.**

**In conjunction with Jobs Partnership we have developed ShineWorks employee training and the Shine: Next Level Leadership development program.**

For over twenty years Jobs Partnership has been preparing people for life and work using Biblical principles. At Jobs Partnership, we come alongside workers and provide practical training, helpful relationships, and resources to prepare people for jobs that offer career advancement.

Through LifeWorks and ShineWorks training, Jobs Partnership is transforming how people look at their work. Jobs Partnership's biblically based life skills for work programs offer an innovative combination of virtual and classroom training, coaching/mentoring relationships, and access to resources for career advancement.

Through Jobs Partnership, workers find HOPE:

- Hope Through Relationships
- Opportunity Through Partnerships
- Purpose Through Work
- Empowerment Through Training

**To learn more about Jobs Partnership and our biblically based training solutions, please visit our website at www.jobspartnership.org.**

# SHINE

Matthew 5:16

## SERVE OTHERS
HUMILITY - Put Others First
COMPASSION - Show You Care
GENEROSITY - Exceed Expectations
*Mission of Servanthood*

## HONOR GOD
TRUST - Depend on Him
GRATITUDE - Thank Him
STEWARDSHIP - Serve Him
*Purpose of Faithfulness*

## IMPROVE CONTINUALLY
COMPETENCE - Soar with Strengths
COURAGE - Take Action
PASSION - Empower your Potential
*Vision of Excellence*

## NAVIGATE BY VALUES
CLARITY - Know your Values
CONVICTION - Live your Values
CONFIDENCE - Trust your Values
*Values of Integrity*

## EXCEL IN RELATIONSHIPS
CREDIBILITY - Can I trust you?
PERSEVERANCE - Can I count on you?
LOVE - Do you care about me?
*Impact of Relationships*

"Let your light shine before others, that they may see your good deeds and glorify your Father in heaven."

For a downloadable version visit shinevision.com